the

WAY OF THE
ELDERS

About the Authors

Born of Bamana and Fulani parents in Dakar, Senegal, Adama Kenbougoul Doumbia (Ken for short) grew up in the villages of Senegal and Mali, where he was raised by his elders, who taught him extensively about African traditions and mystical practices. He has since traveled the globe as a master drummer and dancer with internationally renowned companies such as the *Ballet du Senegal* and *Afrique Noire*. Mr. Doumbia has lived in Europe, Asia, and North America, where he has had the opportunity to integrate and contrast his knowledge with other cultures, and, most importantly, recognize the deep significance of teaching and passing down this sacred African wisdom.

With a Ph.D. in comparative philosophy and religion from CIIS, American-born and raised Naomi Doumbia has studied the philosophies and religions of the world and spends most of her time abroad in Africa and Asia writing and conducting research. Through her work, Dr. Doumbia aspires to bring to light the healing and transformative powers of the world's mystical, spiritual traditions.

the

WAY

OF

THE

ELDERS

West African Spirituality & Tradition

ADAMA & NAOMI DOUMBIA Ph.D.

Llewellyn Publications
Saint Paul, Minnesota

FIRST EDITION
First Printing, 2004

Cover design by Ellen Dahl
Drawing on page 87 by Naomi Doumbia
Editing and interior design by Connie Hill
Interior illustrations by Ellen Dahl

Library of Congress Cataloging-in-Publication Data
Doumbia, Adama, 1965–
  The way of the elders: West African spirituality & tradition / Adama
& Naomi Doumbia — 1st ed.
    p.   cm.
  Includes bibliographical references and index.
  ISBN 0-7387-0626-4
  1. Mandingo (African people)—Rites and ceremonies. 2. Mandingo
(African people)—Religion. 3. Mandingo (African people)—Folklore.
4. Africa, West—Social life and customs. I. Doumbia, Naomi, 1971– .
II. Title.

DT474.6.M36D68   2004
299.6'96—dc22   2004057699

Llewellyn Worldwide does not participate in, endorse, or have any authority or responsibility concerning private business transactions between our authors and the public.

All mail addressed to the author is forwarded, but the publisher cannot, unless specifically instructed by the author, give out an address or phone number.

Any Internet references contained in this work are current at publication time, but the publisher cannot guarantee that a specific location will continue to be maintained. Please refer to the publisher's website for links to authors' websites and other sources.

Llewellyn Publications
A Division of Llewellyn Worldwide, Ltd.
P.O. Box 64383, Dept. 0-7387-0626-4
St. Paul, MN 55164-0383, U.S.A.
www.llewellyn.com

Printed in the United States of America

At the feet of our ancestors
To the hands of our children

Contents

INTRODUCTION

Sacred texts of the world's religions serve many of us on our spiritual journeys, offering us guidance, wisdom, and strength in times of challenge and uncertainty. While these scriptures help to satisfy important answers to the deeper questions in life, many of us are not aware of the significant contributions that our ancient, oral, spiritual traditions have to make to our growth and development. Although much of the African spiritual heritage has not been preserved in texts, its sacred wisdom has been passed down orally from our ancestors for thousands of years—even before the advent of the world's major religions as we know them.

The significant advantage of the oral dissemination of a spiritual tradition is that each generation has the opportunity to apply the teachings in a way that responds to the needs of the contemporary community. Thus, African Traditional Religions

(ATR) evolved over millennia, continuously adapting and developing, reflective of the multifarious nature of Spirit itself. The fact that ATR have not been proselytized, forced upon others, or even preserved in written texts, and yet still claim so many adherents worldwide, including the regions of North and South America, is a testimony to its integrity and power.

Some of this ancestral knowledge has been integrated into the practices and beliefs of the newer religions like Christianity and Islam, though many of the customs remain unrecorded. Much of what has been written about religion and spirituality, in general, is presented in the dualistic context of East versus West. African spirituality is often left completely out of the dialogue. So it often is with things deemed too mysterious, fearful, and not easily understood; yet the seeds of many of the world's philosophies and religions sprouted in the fertile and rich metaphysical gardens of the Motherland.

Indeed, there is a whole movement to celebrate this truth with the proliferation of writings about ancient Egypt (Kemet). While the focus on the profound spiritual practices and phenomenal achievements of *ancient* Kemet are significant and necessary to promote, it is important to realize that *contemporary* African culture harbors the existence of a rich and meaningful spiritual tradition, and these contemporary traditions derive from ancient roots. The extraordinary philosophical developments and wisdom of ancient Egypt continue to exist to this very day with abundance in traditions all over Africa. The limited attention that is given to contemporary West Africa focuses mostly on the Yoruba religion.

What little is written by scholars about West African culture has been impeded by language limitations and misinterpretations of African mystical practices. Few truly understand the purpose of spirits or divinities in African life, and the great reverence of the One Spirit. Little is known about the important function of the energy of Spirit, or *nyama*, and its crucial role in the very fabric of daily existence. Many misuse labels such as possession, juju, and fetish to describe African sacred practices. These are all misunderstandings of the deep and powerful expressions of love and devotion for Spirit, humanity, and creation within African cultures.

Truly, there are not any translatable terms to describe these "practices" that are integral to everyday life for West Africans. To bring about rain, cure a disease, or make oneself invisible is not unbelievable or miraculous, as it is often perceived outside of the African world. West Africans live with the understanding that the energy of Spirit permeates everything in nature, and it is within our very reach to work with this exceptional force. Certainly, we can employ this energy for constructive or destructive purposes, but daily interaction with the ancestors, spirits, and Divine energy help to ensure our guided use of this power. Many practicing Christians and Muslims in African societies draw upon this wisdom passed down from the ancestors who taught us about the forces, powers, and spirits that are accessible to us for enhancing the quality of our lives by maintaining our connection with Spirit.

From the birthplace of humanity, this holistic understanding of the inseparability of the physical and spiritual spheres of life has been the foundation of African beliefs since the beginnings of time. What lies at the heart of many of the great Eastern religious traditions, specifically an aspiration toward an extinction of dualistic perceptions and a recognition of the underlying connection of all existence is, in fact, a lived reality for many Africans. It is not an ideal to strive for, a philosophy over which to pontificate or deconstruct, it is an experiential dynamic, an actual way of being.

To grasp this notion of the inseparability of matter and spirit is to shed any linear perceptions of how the universe operates. To understand this concept is to surrender to the idea that all phenomena are interconnected, interrelated, and interdepend-ent—integral parts of a unified whole. To embrace this vision is to acknowledge a vibrant, powerful universe that is not re-ducible to animistic labels, but is a marvel in its variegated, multifaceted manifestation of the One.

Indeed, the most notable feature of ATR is that they simulta-neously uphold oppositions, or what seem like contradictions, honoring the truth that lies in the tension between the two. It is necessary to come from a perspective that is comfortable hold-ing oppositions together, if one is to achieve any insight into African spirituality. This is true for just about every facet of ATR, including the roles of women/men, and magic/science, seeming dualities that, in Africa, are seen as a harmonizing whole. Accordingly, human beings are composed of divinity and, at the same time, honor the Divine through daily worship. Humans are, at once, singular and plural, the individual who worships, a community that worships, and the cosmos that worships, separately and all at once, maintaining an equilibri-um between the singular and whole.

Similarly, both feminine and masculine principles are hon-ored manifestations of the Divine, as are the principles of cre-ation and destruction. Earth-based, fertility-venerating cultures understand that the harmonious cycle of life entails *both* birth and death; they are the natural ebb and flow of life's cycles that are celebrated in the daily rituals of ATR. Thus, Divinity holds both these principles simultaneously and is venerated for it accordingly. Spirit is all powerful and with a swiftness will take life as generously as it gives it.

To be sure, Africa is not homogenous, and there exist great variations in her faiths and customs. At the same time, a commonality in thought and observances persists throughout West Africa, especially among the Mande-populated countries of Mali, Gambia, Guinea, Guinea Bissau, Burkina Faso, Ivory Coast, Senegal, and parts of Liberia, Mauritania, and Sierra Leone.[1] In this book we attempt to collect and write about

The countries of Western Africa are a rich blend of spiritual traditions that integrate many cultural practices. The Mande population extends into several West African countries, as indicated by the shaded area.

some of the cherished beliefs, rituals, ceremonies, and healing practices, with a particular focus on the Bamana (Mande), providing not only a record or catalog, but also a faithful guide to her wisdom.

We do not attempt to offer pure versions of the ancient sacred teachings of the ancestors as passed down from the beginnings of time; colonization and globalization have left their influence and impact on every facet of the culture. This book is rather an attempt to record some of the prevalent existing spiritual beliefs and practices found throughout West Africa. We hope that by providing this written record of these sacred traditions we will promote more awareness, more respect, and more appreciation for the beauty of Africa's gifts to all of us.

I

COSMOS &
NATURE

1
SPIRITS &
ENERGY

Everywhere there is sky, there is Spirit.

Spirit has many names, but there is only one Spirit. Spirit is both near and far, as immanent as the earth and as transcendent as the sky. We recognize the strength and power of the Almighty through a thunderous storm; we feel the reliability and comfort of the Eternal with the rising sun; we observe the grace and beauty of the Creator in a dancing stream. In all of our surroundings, we experience the essence of the Divine. We celebrate Spirit's many qualities apparent or hidden in every form. Each plant, rock, animal, and person tells the story of creation and serves to nurture, teach, and guide us on our life journeys. Our belief that we are all a part of one Spirit affects our relations with one another; the action of one member of the community is felt by every one of us. The ultimate receiver of all prayers, Spirit is always a part of our greetings and blessings. We maintain deep reverence and awe for Spirit.

Spirits

Every spirit belongs to Spirit. We pray to these sacred mediators who share in the Supreme power.[1] Our spiritual well-being is dependent upon our relationship to them; every one of us has the power to commune with these forces through prayer and sacrifice. Before we swim or fish, we make peace with the spirits of the water. Before we hunt or gather wood, we make peace with the spirits of the bush. Before we farm, we make peace with the spirits of the earth. They tell us what kind of sacrifice they desire; each divinity has its own special song, rhythm, color, and sacrificial animal. Sometimes they trouble us when we do not show proper respect to the earth or to one another. If there is too much rain or drought, or any disruption in our environment, we do not attribute it to Spirit but to the divinities to whom we may have not shown proper reverence. Spirits teach us how to bring order, peace, and harmony to our communities.

Some of our spirits lived as human beings; others are forces of nature. They respond to our petitions, though they also operate from their own agendas. If we are unaware of any spirits, they are better able to exercise their own will and roam about freely. The focus of our lives is how effectively to interact with the world of Spirit. They are always communicating their wishes, demands, and prescriptions to us directly, or through our diviners and healers. Divinities draw their power and wisdom from Spirit, and we draw ours from them.

Spirit's Energy

Nyama is the energy that emanates from Spirit and flows throughout the universe.[2] It is the life force that links all of existence together; humans, animals, plants, and minerals. The power of creation and destruction, nyama commands everything from bountiful harvests to droughts and plagues; it directs the twinkling stars and the rippling tides. This energy of the universe shapes nature into its many forms and yields to our handling of its power.

We draw life from this potent force that connects all of creation. It is the fuel for all of our activities. Nyama is the source of energy for every word, thought, and action. To live harmoniously with nature, we live with a sensitivity to the power of nyama. To recognize this energy is to appreciate that everything is interconnected, integral parts of a whole.

Those of us with high levels of nyama, such as shamans, diviners, blacksmiths, bards, and hunters, can maneuver this energy and direct it at will.[3] The ability to channel nyama requires access to advanced levels of mystical knowledge. Those who possess this knowledge hold great influence in our communities. One may devote limitless time and effort to learn how to direct this energy, but most of us leave it to our artisans who inherit large concentrations of nyama from their ancestors. Many of our artisans marry within their own group to maintain their high levels of this energy. One must also learn to handle nyama through intensive training, as it can be deadly if one does not follow the appropriate rituals for engaging it. Our artisans spend their entire lives cultivating their relationship with this power.

Our use of divination, charm making, and herbal healing draws upon our knowledge of this life force. Many of our artisans practice these forms of healing, enhancing and transforming our natural and social environments. Our blacksmiths work with the high levels of this energy present in the iron they shape and the woods they carve for our charms and ritual tools. As words carry power and are full of nyama, our bards possess great skill in directing these high levels of energy through their healing music and storytelling. Our hunters and leather workers handle massive amounts of nyama from the animals they hunt and the skins they treat, which we rely upon for our medicines and protective pieces.

Our awareness of this awesome energy influences our efforts to live in balance and peace with all of Spirit's manifestations. Compassion, love, and selfless acts bring an abundance of this creative energy into our paths and serve to neutralize and keep at bay harmful nyama. Disruptive thoughts and actions can invite disharmony and destruction from this mysterious power. We remain in wonder of this energy of Spirit.

Spirit Visitation

Spirits seldom possess us; they make visits upon us. Spirit visitation is our opportunity to commune with the divinities. We encourage spirit visitation as the whole community prospers when a spirit descends upon one of us. They provide healing and impart knowledge for those of us present. A spirit possesses an individual when it enters one among us uninvited and does not surrender. Spirit possessions may require the intervention of spirit mediums to release the possessing force and divine the reason for the possession. They often occur among those who try to harm others or who neglect to make peace with a particular spirit. Sometimes a divinity may make a surprise visit upon one of us to heal or relay an important message, but most of the time the spirits wait for our invitations.

We may construct a special altar for a spirit, in the form of a shrine, if it begins to visit regularly and offer guidance and support. We keep the shrine in a ceremonial room or in our home and offer regular libations and prayers to keep it content and comfortable.

Preparations

Before spirit visitation, those among us ready to receive a spirit must enter a fully open and meditative state, surrendering all expectations, needs, and desires. We clean ourselves, bathing with protective herbs to keep at bay unwanted forces. Frankincense is a common herb we burn at these ceremonies to ward off disruptive spirits. We also make a brew of protective herbs that no one at the ceremony may know, except the diviner who prepares them. We might wear special clothes to show our readiness to receive the spirit. We sometimes mark sacred symbols on our bodies with white chalk or clay, and wear powerful charms to strengthen us when the divinity visits. We may put white powder on our face and body to foster purity and well-being. We also prepare the ceremonial area with perfumes and water. The divinities enjoy the sweet smells and feel welcomed by our gifts. We may carry special herbs in a pot of water or place the shrines themselves on top of our heads to help bring on the visitation.

Ceremony

Performing rituals and making sacrifices encourage the spirit's power and benevolence. We pour libations of palm wine, millet beer, or water. Our prayers and incantations include blessings for the members of the group, and an invitation of a spirit to the ceremony to perform revelations, wondrous transformations, and healing. We sacrifice an animal such as a chicken or a goat. We may sprinkle the blood of the animal on the shrine, or we may cut out the liver of the animal and offer it up on the shrine. Usually, we consume the meat of the sacrifice and the beverage of the libations, creating a unity among all of us and the spirit.

We continue our prayers and communicate with the spirit through our music and dance. Sometimes we play a specific drum rhythm, which will encourage a particular spirit's visitation. The drumming, chanting, and dancing may include everyone present at the ceremony. Our ceremonies can last several hours or several days.

Spirit Communion

Once the spirit descends, we speak and move in the manner of it, communicating its message to the community. When the spirit visits, we are not fully aware of what is happening; our voices may change, and our bodies may move and shake from the power of the divinity's presence. We may do things we would not ordinarily do as we become fully inhabited by the visiting spirit who has its own unique personality. We usually cannot make regular conversation or eye contact. We lose our vision of this world, and develop an inner vision. Some of us begin to speak a different language. Someone present will interpret the message from the spirit. When the divinity serves its purpose and departs, the visited among us often experience complete serenity and joy.

Ancestors

Our ancestors are the closest to us of all the intermediary spirits; they are our guardian spirits. Our ancestors maintain their role in our families and lives, more significantly than when they were physically present. They are always available to us, offering their guidance and protection.

With other divinities, we must first learn their particular language and preferred sacrifice to communicate with them. With our ancestors, we already speak their language; we know their preferences and wishes. At times, when we are neglectful or unaware, they send us signals to capture our attention. They teach us to know Spirit everywhere hidden behind the appearance of things.

We pray for our ancestors and we perform sacrifice to honor their lives. We appreciate them for the life they gave us and the ways they continue to instruct and nurture us. They provide us with our names, our trades, and our knowledge. Every family receives its own set of rules and teachings from its ancestors.

Before each meal, we may place a piece of food on the ground as we call out the name of an ancestor. Friday is a special day when they like to eat with us. We may set aside a portion of food for them on this day, or we leave food out Thursday evening if they come overnight. Whenever we drink, we spill a little on the ground for them. We always serve a drink to the ancestors before posing a question or making a request of them.

We may offer them their favorite foods, such as porridge, and pour it onto the earth and pray. They especially prefer when we offer balls of millet cakes. Libations of alcohol, such as millet beer, are another ancestral favorite. We give kola nuts, biscuits, and sugar away for offerings. We sacrifice a red or white chicken, and let the blood run into the soil and pray. As our ancestors have become one with the light, they especially like hats and shoes, which protect them from the brightness that surrounds them. We give away these items to people as offerings for our ancestors.

We set up stones as altars for our ancestors and place them near our homes, in our yards, and in the center of the village. Sometimes we pray and make sacrifice where our ancestors lived or where they prayed. Often before we pray, we will chew pieces of kola nut, which we spit out onto their altar. The juice of the kola nut tempers our speech and ensures its purity and integrity.

There is no formula to our prayer; we pray from our hearts. We talk with our ancestors as we do with those among us who are physically present. We ask them to work on our behalf in the world of Spirit. The most important way we honor our ancestors is how we live; they are always watching us. Sometimes our ancestors come to live among us, to help us through our children. The ways our children look or act reveal to us who they may be.

Animal Spirits

Animal spirit comes to us as a protective divinity, preserving the village from poverty, hunger, and illness.[4] This spirit also shields our community from harmful nyama and disruptive mystical practices. Animal spirits may come in the form of any animal, like a goat, donkey, lizard, snake, or horse. They sometimes come in the form of a tree, though they are usually able to transform themselves into some kind of an animal.

These creatures generally do not like the light and dwell in caves, forests, or mountains, though they remain near to the village. In every village, one will make itself known and we will often give it a special name. Usually we honor one specific creature, but sometimes we may honor all animals of its kind. Many times it will possess special powers. In one village, a snake might change into many different colors and have no end to its length.

Once an animal spirit makes itself known to the community, one must never harm or kill it, or members of its kind, as this can bring about destructive consequences.[5] Entire villages have been known to burn down through the unintentional harming of the animal spirit, if a sacrifice was not immediately performed to appease it. Sometimes a family will have a special animal spirit that tells a story of the family's ancestors. The family will never eat or harm any incarnation of its divinity.

We make a yearly sacrifice to our animal spirit, and we may also make visits to its dwelling place to thank it for a bountiful harvest. Our elders know where to make the sacrifice and what kind to make. In some villages only the elders are present during the ceremony, and in other villages everyone participates. Each house may provide a sacrifice to an elder who will make the offering to the animal spirit. Sometimes everyone in the village will cook and eat the sacrifice together.

Each animal has its own sacrifice that it likes. Elders may offer a live chicken or goat that they house in the abode of the

animal spirit for it to consume. They offer prayers for the con-
tinuance of peace and abundance within the community. A ceremony may last up to three days.

Sometimes a woman who is experiencing difficulties conceiving a child may visit the spirit's site to offer porridge, kola
nuts, or chicken blood to the animal. A person may make a sacrifice of an animal to secure a husband or wife. We teach our
children at a young age what the animal looks like so they will
not harm it. Animal spirits teach us to have respect for nature
and all her creatures.

Story of the Animal Spirit

Many of our family names come from our relationship to a particular animal spirit. A protective animal spirit of the Diara family is the lion (*diara* means "lion"). Snakes protect the Cissé,
Niaré, Dramé, and Doukouré families, and crocodiles watch
over the Traoré and Mariko lineages. The elephant oversees the
Samaké family (*sama* means "elephant"). Doumbia's animal
spirit is the tiger, and members of this family are not to wear
tiger-print clothing, nor harm this animal.

Couloubaly is a common Mande name with a rich story behind its origination.[6] Couloubaly, or *kulun-bali*, means "no boat
is there." This name comes from a special time, long ago, when a
king and his younger brother ruled a quiet little community on
the edge of the river. The people lived peacefully until, one day,
a nearby kingdom threatened to overtake them. The neighboring army moved in quickly and overpowered the village inhabitants, but the two king brothers were able to escape to the back
of the village at the river. When they reached the edge of the
water, the two men had no boat to cross and the army was

quickly closing in to capture them. The brothers were trapped, when suddenly a huge catfish came to the edge of the river, just in time. The two kings jumped on the fish and were escorted across the river to safety. From this day forward, the Couloubaly brothers promised this animal spirit that no one from their clan would ever harm or consume any catfish.

Bush Spirits

Spirits of the bush are mostly benevolent; few are harmful. One must always show proper reverence to these powerful forces who can transform themselves into anything they wish to serve their purposes.[7] Bush spirits only fear the lion, which is able to consume them. Bush spirits are blind to these domineering creatures, so they like to befriend those of us who frequent their domain. They give us knowledge about the wilderness, and in exchange, we show them where the lions roam. When family members do not return home, after they visit the bush, we know that these divinities have taken them. Those among us who return from a long stay in the forest often possess mystical and healing powers. Bush spirits are available to offer us their help, guidance, and wisdom in the domain of the wild. Often they are capricious, but this only serves to keep us alert and bring us greater awareness and discernment of our environment.

We access these spirits through divination, visitation, or music. They especially enjoy bright colors and large gatherings of people. We sometimes recognize these spirits in the market-place, as they often buy only vegetables and never bargain on the price. Bush spirits will not eat hot food, but they enjoy eating food that was cooked the day before. We believe that eating leftover food brings one a long life; it is full of nyama and has the blessings of being consumed by the ancestors and other spirits.

Although very independent, bush spirits will serve those of us who invoke them with special formulas we inherit from our ancestors. Our ancestors made pacts with these divinities since the beginnings of time, consisting of prohibitions and obligations, which we and the spirits continue to honor.

Story of the Bush Spirit

There was a time, long ago, when we lived together with the bush spirits. We shared our food and what little money we had. As our community was quite large, with spirits and humans sharing everything, there was not enough food for everyone. We decided, one day, that we would farm to grow more food. We let the bush spirits decide what we were going to plant. Everything that grew above the ground, the bush spirits told us we could keep for ourselves; everything that was left underneath the earth they would take for themselves.

The first year, we grew corn and that corn stretched high up into the sky. Since we were to have everything above the ground, we kept the corn, and the bush spirits took the roots from the earth. This agreement did not help the bush spirits much, as they were not as successful at selling their roots in the marketplace as we were at selling our corn.

The second year, the bush spirits decided that we would grow peanuts. This time, they planned to take what grew above the ground, and we were to take what grew below it. At the end of the harvest, the bush spirits came and cut all of the peanut leaves and tried to sell them, unsuccessfully. We took all of our peanuts and, once again, prospered selling them in the market-place. The bush spirits were troubled. Before the sun set, the cries of the bush spirits could be heard across the mountain tops. This was the last time the bush spirits lived together with us.

Lessons of the Bush Spirit Story

We teach our children the story of the bush spirit to help them understand our whimsical relationship with these divinities. We were close to the bush spirits like a family in the past, but we now have a relationship of competition and rivalry. As human beings, we have a special connection with the earth and we learned quickly how to receive her gifts and nourishment. We may have been more clever than the bush spirits for tilling the land and growing our crops, but the bush spirits own the wilderness where they have since made their home. When we are in their territory, we are subject to their ways and must show them proper respect.

Crossroads' Spirits

The crossroads' spirit is the spirit of change, transformation, and protection. We pay homage to this power at any crossroads we encounter by leaving behind some type of offering. In the village, we make regular offerings at the crossroads to honor the founding of the village. We also break eggs at an intersection when we experience challenges in our lives. One must not look back afterward, or the offering will not work. Breaking eggs, a symbol of fertility and potential growth, is a statement to the spirit that one is ready to invite positive change into one's life.

We may also clean ourselves with water and herbs at the cross-roads, to help us overcome difficult transitions. Women dance *moribiassa* at the crossroads to petition this divinity for the healing of a loved one who is ill or experiencing mental challenges. They will wear men's clothes as they dance this rhythm, and then leave the clothes behind as an offering.

We also cover an animal tail with cowries and herbal medi-cine and dip it into water to sprinkle on us for healing at the crossroads. When we have accidentally killed an animal, we may appease the animal's nyama by soaking the animal in water and bathing with this water at the junction. This act of humility shows the animal's spirit our remorse, and enables the spirit to cross over peacefully. The crossroads' spirit teaches us the im-portance of accepting change and generating change that is peaceful and harmonious.

Dwarf Spirits

The month of August is the time of the dwarf spirits. The dwarf spirits may come at anytime, but they especially like to visit after the big rain when there is an abundance of vegetables and food. They like the full moon as well and usually roam about during this magical time. Dwarf spirits are wise, though mis-chievous, spirits of the bush, who usually dwell near anthills, baobab, or banana trees which provide them with their favorite foods.[8] They enjoy eating couscous, so we often sprinkle hot sauce on top of this dish so they will not eat this food that we leave out for our ancestors. Peanuts are also a favorite snack.

These feisty creatures particularly like to surprise us, trick us, and steal food from our homes. We know them by their small height and backwards feet. They may also wear red beards and grow long fingernails. Dwarf spirits are mostly harmless spirits, but they will fight for their food, which they collect in the calabash they carry. We say that the one who obtains the calabash of a dwarf spirit will never be poor. Like the magic lamp of a genie, the spirit of this magical calabash will grant any wish to its possessor. It is also an almost impossible task to retrieve this auspicious calabash from a dwarf spirit.

These little creatures often run from homes with dogs, which can give them away. We dress our children with large hats if they need to go out at night to protect them from the dwarf spirits; the hats make them look taller and keep the dwarf spirits from coming to play with them. Dwarf spirits are also known to mimic the voice of the herders to steal cattle; they especially enjoy drinking cow's milk. Herders often have a special ability to see these little creatures who also like to run off with our horses and donkeys to tend to their business.

Dwarf spirits possess great knowledge about plants and medicine, too, and will share this special information with a few of us. They teach us valuable things about the bush and represent a playful quality of Spirit. Dwarf spirits keep us on our toes, vigilant and unassuming.

Human Spirits

One of our goals as human beings is to gracefully harmonize matter and spirit. We contain within each of us an element of all existing things, connecting us to every creature and making us interdependent with creation. Our diverse qualities make us the center of attraction for many kinds of forces. Our ancestors and elders, through ritual, prayer, sacrifice, and initiation teach us how to balance the power and energy within us. When one among us is not balanced, this attracts harmful spirits into our path and disrupts the harmony of the entire community.

Some of us have disturbed spirits that can cause great harm to others. We believe these unruly spirits leave their bodies in the night to break down and consume the life of others. The departed bodies of these intrusive forces cannot be awakened when they leave on their mission. They have the appetite to make others ill and disappear. This hereditary power resides in the gut of a person and grows stronger with age. These people have the ability to change their appearances and travel great distances. We say they have eyes in the backs of their heads as they can see everything around them. They ravish the hearts of people and pass the spoils on to others. Those of us who can see them, see them walking on their heads. We describe them as creatures who possess qualities that are upside down or backward. They represent those forces that serve to undermine the structure and unity we strive for within our communities.

These spirits reside mostly in women, but sometimes they dwell in men too.[9] It is the women among us who have the power to protect us from them, as they are best at seeing these people with troubled spirits. They provide herbs to keep them away or make them lose their power by convincing them to confess to their actions. Those of us who feel attacked by such spirits burn cotton seeds, frankincense, and kunjé (*Guiera senegalensis*) together and inhale the fumes. This concoction of herbs provides a protective shield around us and keeps these spirits at bay.

2
OFFERINGS &
SACRIFICE

*Be careful what you throw into the
"pool of life" because of the ripples
that inevitably result.*

Offerings and sacrifice serve as our communication, prayers, and gifts to the spirits. They can be something we make in a time of crisis or something we perform daily to ensure harmony and peace within our families and communities. We use them to make amends and requests, or to show gratitude for all of our blessings.

When we make an offering or sacrifice, we give up something that has significance for us in our daily lives. These honorable acts teach us the value of what we have and what we are able to share. We learn from our offerings and sacrifice the true meaning of our blessings. This cultivates our humility and gratitude, which invites more blessings our way. Sometimes we give our offerings to the spirits directly, sometimes we give them to people in honor of the spirits. We give that which brings joy to others. We give to others and they pray on our behalf. When people are content and their bellies full, their hearts are warmed and their prayers are sweet.

We never speak of our offerings or sacrifices. Speaking and boasting defeats the purpose of the gift and is more harmful to us than if we had given nothing at all. If our offerings do not foster more modesty and appreciation, they are meaningless.

We often make an offering or sacrifice to amend our disruptive ways. If we harm those in our communities, creatures in our environment, or elements of nature, we make an offering to appease the nyama of the transgression. When one harms any member of the community or any living being, including plants and animals, one must make the appropriate offering to atone for the violation.

We pay close attention to the messages from the spirits about the kinds of sacrifice and offerings we need to make and how often we need to make them. If we ignore a message from the spirits, the communication will only persist, with increasing power, until we acknowledge it. Often the message will come through the loss, theft, or destruction of a valuable item. We observe closely the manner in which things are taken from us, and note the distinction of whether they are missing, stolen, or destroyed. Often when we lose or misplace something, it is a sign from the spirits that we need to make some kind of offering. Sometimes when we lose something precious, it will at once resurface after we make the appropriate offering. If not, we understand that the item itself was the required offering.

Something stolen sometimes reflects as much on the owner as the thief. Perhaps the item was something we were not to have in the first place, or it was obtained in an unwholesome way. The item could contain harmful nyama from a previous owner and was therefore seized immediately from us for safety and forewarning. In all instances, a theft is a warning that we need to more carefully observe our surroundings and beware of our indiscretions.

When an item is destroyed it is also a great opportunity for us to examine our values and conduct. If something is destroyed, it is a powerful message that this item was simply not meant to be in our possession any longer. Perhaps it was overly valued and, therefore, harmful for the owner. In our communities, when we receive a valuable gift, we are often relieved when it receives a tear or scratch or something that devalues it. We then say that the nyama has been released from the item and we no longer have to worry that it holds so much importance for us.

We strive in our communities to maintain a genuine lack of attachment to things in this world, as such attachments distract us from the world of Spirit. Nothing in this life is more important than our relationship with Spirit, and any behavior or attitude that places anything before Spirit will surely attract lessons to correct it. Spirits are most desirous of those things that we wish to possess and will not hesitate to compete with us for them. We truly own nothing in this life, and the spirits are more than willing to teach us this lesson as often as we need.

When we find ourselves dropping or spilling food or other items, we see this as a sign to make an offering or sacrifice. If we find ourselves in accidents or dangerous situations, we heed this as a warning for making sacrifice. If one of us falls ill in the community, this is an obvious call for sacrifice.

Friday is the best day to make an offering or sacrifice, as it is the end of the work week, and a time of festivity when the ancestors and spirits like to visit with us. Wednesday evening, the middle of the week, is also a favorable time. Monday, the start of the work week, is a heavy day, and not auspicious for making offerings or sacrifice.

Animal Sacrifice

The most popular kind of sacrifice we make in our communities is the slaying of an animal.[1] We pray before we sacrifice an animal, and we perform the act swiftly and humanely, so that Spirit will receive it. When we slay an animal, the cut to the throat must be clean and quick to minimize the suffering of the animal; otherwise, the sacrifice is not honorable. We then cook every part of the animal so that there is not any waste. We give a portion of the meat to as many families as we can. The more families who enjoy the sacrifice, the more people there are to pray on our behalf.

Animal sacrifice is one of the most powerful sacrifices we make because it contains the sacred fluid of blood. Carrying the life-force throughout every living being, blood is a substance full of nyama. The shedding of blood makes way for new life, new beginnings. The fluid of fertility, rebirth, and life, blood is the ultimate offering to the spirits. It is the only part of the sacrifice we do not consume ourselves, but save for the spirits' consumption. We let the blood run deep into the earth, nourishing that by which it has been nourished.

Chickens are our most common sacrifice. Sheep, goats, and cows are popular too, but we usually save these larger animals for grand occasions, such as naming ceremonies, childhood initiations, marriages, and funerals. We may sacrifice chickens to empower our personal charms, or to help remove obstacles that cross our paths. We usually slay only the male animals, and we never eat animals that we find dead. To eat a pregnant animal is forbidden.

To know if a sacrifice is pure, we open up the heart of the slain animal. If the heart is full of dark blood, the person who has slain the animal has an unlit heart. If the heart is not full of blood, we know that the sacrifice is pure and the spirits will receive it. We believe that the spirits consume the essence or life of the food or libations we give to them.

Standard Offerings

Many of our standard offerings include white objects, such as sugar, milk, or paper, which symbolize the purity of the gifts we give. They also represent some of the staples in our communities, things upon which we rely and that hold value for us. Our most common offering is a porridge and sauce.[2] Porridge consists of a cooked grain and the sauce we may make as a separate offering. We cook a grain such as millet and add yogurt, milk, and sugar to it, creating a sweet dish that we serve at almost all of our ceremonies and give away or consume on many different occasions. We make creative varieties of this dish, sometimes adding honey, peanut butter, or other sweet flavors or seasonings.

Libations

Anytime one drinks any liquor, one spills a little on the ground as an offering to the ancestors. Palm wine and millet beer are our most common alcoholic libations. We may also offer red wine as a substitute for blood when we do not have an animal available to us for sacrifice. We pour milk or water for libations too.

Church, Mosque, or Temple Offerings

We may make offerings to members of our place of worship, who pray on our behalf. Any offering is acceptable, but the most common items we give away are money, kola nuts, candles, sugar, or pots of cooked food for the community. If we belong to a congregation of worshippers, we often make our offerings or sacrifices on special holidays.

Street Offerings

One way we make an offering is to give something to a stranger on the street. For our street offerings, we may give away white sugar, white paper, white yogurt, biscuits, white candles, kola nuts, or money. When we present gifts to strangers, they know to pray for us. They may simply nod when they receive our offering and continue on their way, or they say a short prayer for the gift, such as "that Spirit give you what you need." We may make this kind of offering for the ancestors, family members who have fallen ill, or to overcome any challenges in our lives.

3
SHAMANS: DIVINERS & HEALERS

*The secret belongs to the one who knows
how to keep silent.*

The role of the shaman in our communities is great.
Shamans are our doctors and spiritual leaders; the
two are not separate for us. Any illness, pain, or suffering is the manifestation of a spiritual wound or
challenge. Our shamans help us to identify why we
are suffering, who or what may be at the cause of it,
and what exactly we need to do to remedy it. We use
many names to describe all of the different specialists in our communities who provide numerous
kinds of divination and healing. Among these specialists, their roles often overlap. All of our shamans
work with nyama and spirits to heal members of
our communities.

Diviners: Those Who See

Those of us who *see* use many objects in nature to aid us in our divination. We examine the configurations of tossed cowrie shells.[1] We observe the designs drawn in the sand. We speak with bush spirits who may visit us regularly and offer messages about members of the community. We communicate with our loved ones away on a journey through the water in a new calabash. We interpret signs such as the movements of snakes. We listen carefully to the whistles of birds. We burn special herbal leaves and place the ashes outside for the wind to blow them in certain directions, which provide answers to our questions.

We employ special charms for divination. A common charm we use is a bull's tail, which we tie with cotton thread and small pieces of straw. We wrap the tail in a red sack, sometimes decorated with cowrie shells. This powerful charm has many purposes, including helping our diviners to see. Some of us fill up baskets with bones, teeth, fingernails, claws, seeds, and stones, that we rattle until the spirit comes and speaks through them. Any diviner among us will usually use more than one method of divination to confirm the message.

Our diviners use these many methods to help those of us in the community with our concerns and challenges. When doubts, disagreements, or misfortunes visit us, we may consult with a diviner to understand the origins and nature of our issues. We may look to a diviner for direction on travel, work, or potential mates. Diviners help us see not only what may be obstructions to our path, but also blessings to come. Our diviners enable us to communicate with the realm of the spirits and with our ancestors, to determine whether or not we are on our correct spiritual paths and fulfilling our true destinies.

We consult our diviners at any time for a multitude of purposes; however, Friday is not the best day for diviners to perform a reading, as we reserve this special day for prayer and sacrifice to the spirits. We hold great respect for our diviners, and are conscious to never cross their paths without proper acknowledgment.

Calabash Readings

Calabash readings are the most common method for communicating with the spirit of loved ones who are away on journey. We also, at times, use this method to communicate with those who have crossed over. We place special herbs inside a calabash and say a prayer to invite the person to appear in the water. Only the diviner knows the secret herbs to use for this powerful form of divination. Sometimes a diviner may pour palm wine into the calabash and invite the spirit to communicate. The spirits speak with us, relaying important messages, or assuring us of their well-being.

Cowrie Shell Readings

Cowrie shell divination is a popular form of divination. The diviner usually tosses twelve shells onto a mat to read. Sometimes diviners toss twenty or forty shells, and a diviner often adds a coin or two along with the shells as an offering to bless the reading. We remove the backs, or the round side of the cowries, to balance them so they will land equally on either side.

Our diviners read the patterns in the shells after a toss. Sometimes there is no pattern, and the diviner will quickly round the shells up in one hand and toss them out again. It is mostly the shells that land together that are meaningful to the diviner; however, all diviners read the patterns differently. When a configuration reads health, longevity, and prosperity, we call this reading *wassa*.

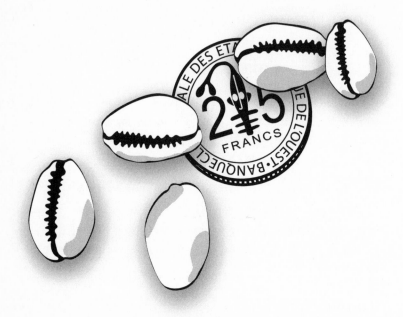

Cowrie shells are tossed onto a mat and read by the diviner. The coin serves as an offering to bless the reading.

Kola Nut Readings

The most customary way to practice kola nut divination is to read how the kola nuts land after we toss them. There are many different interpretations of the configuration of tossed kola nuts. One interpretation reads that if a kola nut is split into four parts when it hits the ground, the individual may make their request. If all of the four pieces of the kola fall on the round of their backs, or if all of them land on their flat surfaces with their faces to the ground, then the reply is favorable. If two of the kola pieces land with their round backs up and two of them land face-downward, then the reply is also favorable. If three pieces of the kola fall with their faces to the ground, or with their faces upward, the reply is unfavorable.

The rounded and flat sides of kola nuts have significance when used in divination.

Prayer Bead Readings

Muslims among us see with the ninety-nine beads of Spirit's name. A person with an inquiry or challenge will select one bead from the necklace. The diviner will then write down the name of the bead and study it overnight. The inquirer will receive information about his or her particular concern the following day. The best time to check is on Thursday night.

Sand Readings

A favorite form of divination is sand reading. A pile of sand is smoothed out flatly on a surface. The diviner may take a moment for a brief period of meditation. Some diviners tilt back their heads and close their eyes, others divine with open eyes and focus. The diviner traces a couple of long, horizontal zigzags in the sand, and then begins to punctuate them with short, vertical lines. The short, vertical lines tell the diviner about the client's situation. Through careful examination of the lines, the diviner can see where there is disharmony and what may be the necessary remedy. The specific configurations of short, vertical lines make up much of the sacred writing of our charms.

Healers

Healers among us receive a great amount of respect and support for the blessings they provide us. For illness, natural disasters, disharmony in the household, grief among friends, or any irregularity or upheaval, the healer has the remedy. Often, one may visit a diviner first to determine the nature or root of a situation. The diviner will then either recommend the appropriate remedy, such as a sacrifice or prayer, or will direct one to a specific healer in the community who can produce the best solution.

As these shamans are in constant communion with the spirits, they have access to most any information or power we may request of them. They often work with large quantities of nyama, and can, at times, affect the growth of a crop or even the cessation of rain from the sky. Rainmaking, charm creating, and illness curing are among some of the many tasks our shamans perform for us. If they are not effective, we will not call upon them again. One must establish a record of success before developing a reputation as a healer.

Many of our healers are most knowledgeable about plants and animals, providing us with our herbal remedies and charm ingredients. There is not an individual among us who possesses all the information in this area, but there are those among us who are more skilled in these sciences than the rest. One must know where to locate certain plants, the times of their harvest, and all of the uses of each part of them, including the flowers, fruits, leaves, stems, barks, roots and seeds. One is often familiar with the hides, furs, feathers, claws, teeth, shells, eggs, and organs of the different animals. Our mystical practitioners know to what purpose and in what combination one must use these ingredients for healing or charm making.

We possess countless recipes and instructions for the use of these materials to accomplish almost any goal or activity. Our recipes enable us to treat all kinds of illness and ailments. We also keep instructions for the creation of any kind of charm, which can bring protection, success, and anything one desires. Using these recipes wisely is what distinguishes a healer from an individual who may use these recipes to harm others or to gain material things at the expense of others. Healers are sensitive to the balance of life and nature and understand that using recipes that upsets this balance will surely have nyamic repercussions on the community. Everyone suffers from harmful brews and charms; such things produce feelings of ill will and often revenge.

Individuals may purchase recipes from our healers that include the ingredients and their proper use. The recipes may also contain special prayers, chants, and other offerings or sacrifices one must make to the spirits. One purchases a recipe by offering something in exchange for it. An offering is what an individual can give, it is not what one must pay. This can include anything from money or clothes to food or animals. A recipe will not work without an offering in exchange. Maintaining the proper balance for this exchange is important, and, in order to receive something of value, one must be willing to make an offering for it.

Many of our practitioners possess special recipes that they keep only for themselves or their families. Obtaining a collection of recipes to heal others takes time, energy, and resources. Many of us leave this undertaking to our healers who come from shaman families or who heed a calling from the spirits to provide this service. By possessing so much power in our communities, our shamans are vulnerable to competitive spirits and individuals who may challenge them.

Many of these mystical practitioners are our artisans, who transform natural objects into products for our protective charms, ritual, and ceremony. The artisans among us also share the common bond of working with nyama. They will often offer us guidance on the types of offering or sacrifice we need to make to appease disruptive nyama.

Bards

Praise of the Word
It excites or calms souls.
The word is total:
it cuts, excoriates
forms, modulates

perturbs, maddens
cures or directly kills
amplifies or reduces
According to intention
It excites or calms souls.

—Praise song of a bard of
the Bamana Komo society

Bards are preservers of our values and social customs; they are our professional historians and storytellers.[2] These "masters of the word" retain the stories of our families and chronicle, analyze, and interpret our traditions. As the counselors of kings, they committed to memory the history of the kingdoms. Now every family has its own bard who preserves the family's history. Bards retain everything of our heritage by memory. Masters of elaborate verbal, musical, and memory skills, they can recite long stories, epics, and praise poems celebrating our legacy. Each performer of a new generation improvises, adding new reflections to the stories.

The depth of our bards' ancestral knowledge imbues them with vast amounts of nyama. We say that the power of the words from the mouth of a bard can split open a door or make the leaves fall off a tree. The mouth carries some of the highest concentrations of nyama in the body. It is the entry point for sustenance and potential poisons through air and food; it is the exit point for everything one knows, thinks, and believes. Bards are "owners of the mouth" and possess a strong ethical and spiritual ability to control the nyama of the spoken or sung word. Through story, song, and music, these artists of verbal energy heal those among us with grieving hearts and troubled spirits. They uplift us with their encouragement, comfort us with their insights, and inspire us through their mastery of the word.

Blacksmiths

Smiths produce many of the tools for our work, play, defense, ceremony, and ritual. They are our inventors who foster deep and important relationships with the spirits. We maintain a high level of respect for their power to transform and create sacred objects for fertility, healing, rainmaking, divination, and prophesy. The smiths' contact with these powerful objects equips them with high levels of nyama, enabling them to heal without the objects themselves. Smiths are also the village doctors and surgeons, performing the sacred act of circumcision. They often possess a vast amount of knowledge of herbal medicines and treatments as well. They are masters of ceremonies and belong to the most powerful secret societies.

The ancestor of our blacksmiths was close to the spirit of fire.[3] He learned the important act of how to extract iron and transform it into tools and sacred objects for our daily activities and worship; we use this precious metal when we cook, hunt, till the soil, and arm ourselves. [4] We often construct our shrine ornaments and charms from it. Some of our protective pieces contain metals we wear as rings, bracelets, and belts, which harbor high levels of nyama.

The workplace of our smiths, the forge, is the sacred space where they work to control the nyama of the metal. The forge is where all four elements of creation operate in harmony and balance: fire, air, water, and earth. With the four elements present, smiths are at their best to harness the nyama for the creation of tools, art, and ritual objects.

Smiths begin their workday with meditation and sacrifice. Infertile women may come to sit at the sacred forge during the morning meditations to receive the potent levels of nyama to remedy their condition. A woman who experienced a challenging childbirth will wear an iron necklace with a tiny pair of smith tongs as a pendant for future births.

Smiths are also our woodcarvers. They create many of our ritual masks and sculptures, which receive high levels of their nyama. To sanctify the wood for these objects, the smith must carefully select the appropriate tree on a specific day. Normally, on the first day of the new moon, the smith sacrifices a chicken whose blood, mixed with chewed-up kola nuts, is poured on to the tree to appease the tree's nyama. Mondays and Thursdays are auspicious days for a smith to commence the carving of a ritual object.

Smiths may lead invocations, dances, songs, and praises to bring about successful creations. They sometimes place prohibitions on their workers' sexual contact, to keep pure the nyama of the creation. A smith may commission an uncircumcised boy to help shape a ritual piece so that it receives the purity and higher levels of nyama the boy possesses.

Smiths and hunters share their own special relationship, as the smith supplies the hunter with the necessary weapons and protective charms for his work in the bush. The smith imbues these tools with potent levels of nyama, ensuring the hunter of safety and success in the wilderness.

Hunters

Hunters spend their lives working in the realm of wilderness animals and spirits. To be successful, a hunter must learn how to use his own nyama and direct the nyama of the bush. An animal's nyama can bring famine, sickness, or death to the one who harms or kills it. The hunter must increase his own levels of nyama to protect himself from the animals he kills. The hunter learns about the different plants and animals of the forest and how to use this knowledge to be a healer as well as a hunter.

Hunters will wear powerful clothing and objects to protect them during their hunt. Mud cloth is a sacred garment our hunters wear for protection and identification.[5] Women stain pieces of cotton with herbal leaves and bark and design sacred symbols on the fabric with mud. The whole process is long and demanding and imbues the clothing with potent levels of nyama. Hunters also wear objects that contain great concentrations of nyama such as animal bones, claws, skins, horns, shells, and metal pieces to protect them on their missions. They will also carry their special charms, of which only they know the contents. The hunter may wear his charm on his belt or hung about his shoulder.

One way a hunter may absorb the nyama of the slain animal is to bathe in the blood of the animal while praying that the animal's spirit will bear no ill will. Strong and large animals possess potent levels of nyama, and hunters who kill them obtain more levels of this energy. When a hunter kills an animal, he may dance the movements of that animal in a village ceremony. By engaging a certain kind of dance, he breaks the nyama of the slain animal.

Another method for ensuring a successful hunt and appeasing the nyama of the wild is for the hunter to inhale an herbal mixture. The hunter may mix the fat of a few slain animals along with some herbs, and place hot coals on the grease to create clouds of thick medicinal smoke. The hunter sits at the pot, inhaling the fumes, at the same time calling out the spirit he is invoking.

Sanènè and Kontron are two popular spirits that our hunters often invoke for their help and protection in the wilderness. Sanènè and Kontron are feminine and masculine spirits and, together, represent the balanced forces of nature. Our hunters tell many stories of the two spirits whose relationship changes from mother and son, sister and brother, to wife and husband. Hunters often construct altars to these spirits in the bush where they pour libations and offer up millet and kola nuts. Hunters sometimes place the written names of these divinities inside their charms for protection and prosperous hunting.

4
CHARMS:
AMULETS & TALISMANS

One cannot always kneel at the altar—
but the statue can.

—Dogon proverb

It is a rare individual among us who does not retain a charm for protection or well-being. Amulets are the most popular type of charms that we wear, and serve to keep away illness, trouble, and unwanted spirits. Talismans are charms that bring us prosperity, relationships, and whatever we desire. For every human need or want, we can construct a charm to satisfy it. However, if we commission a charm that is harmful to others or is excessive in its goal, then the charm will require a high spiritual price most of us do not want to pay. Spirits may grant whatever we desire, but they always require something in return. We make sacrifices and offerings for our charms of protection, but when we desire material wealth, power, or prestige we must pay with an equal amount of energy. One who wishes to obtain great fame or fortune may give up a finger, toe, or even a limb. Some may even agree to give up a child. These instances are rare in our communities, but known to all of us.

The nyama or energy of any undertaking demands a comparable payment. We are conscious in our lives to maintain fairness and balance in our transactions with others, monetary or otherwise, as the person who benefits more ultimately pays. If a merchant sells an overpriced item, the nyama of the transaction will ultimately exact revenge on the merchant.[1] We are sensitive to the benefits of giving more and receiving less.

It is the charm makers and artisans among us who create the charms to provide to members of our communities. We prefer those who possess potent levels of nyama and high spiritual knowledge to construct our charms, as this makes them most effective. Our newborns will begin life wearing some charm about the neck, wrist, or waist. To the ripe old age of our elders, all of us continue to renew and multiply our life charms.

Charm Ingredients

In preparation, we find the most suitable objects energetically to match our intentions for our charms. Ancestral pieces, including samples of their clothing, locks of hair, or fingernails, are some of the most charged ingredients for our charms. The fingernails and hair of powerful shamans and diviners are also desirable.

Animal products, such as claws, feathers, bones, and hair, are basic ingredients for our charms. We may place the compo-

This charm or amulet, made of a black goat's hair, is worn around the waist as protection against disruptive people or bush spirits, who may try to hinder one's work.

nents inside animal horns from gazelles or goats. Sacrificial animal blood is an essential ingredient. Chicken eggs contain special powers of abundance. We bury three or seven eggs next to our homes and pray for what we want.

Ashes of certain medicinal plants make powerful ingredients. Gums, spices, and resins seal up our charms. Black salt from the ocean is valuable and we use it for prosperity in our pieces. Lightning droppings found at the base of trees are especially energized. Shells of various types including cowrie, nuts, and snails are favorable additions. Pieces of wood, to which we may attach flowers or beads, are also desirable.

Carrying a little charcoal with salt in one's pouch or pocket protects one from unwanted spirits. Carrying a lime around wards off disquieting spirits. A shower with kolobé (*Combretum micranthum*) herbs protects us against the harmful intentions of others. We wear cowrie shells to make our way clear and to protect us from disruptive spirits and individuals.

Sacred Symbols

Written sacred symbols are an important component of our charms. Traditional sacred symbols represent the spirits of earth, water, fire, and air, and derive from our creation stories. We paint or engrave traditional symbols on our mud-cloth, doors, instruments, and other sacred places inside and outside of the home. These symbols can vary from region to region, but there are basic symbols (below) that most of us recognize.

A capital Y presents the male principle; a capital Y upside down is the female principle. A symmetric X symbolizes human beings and fertility. A symmetric X with a vertical line through the middle of it represents the universe, while a horizontal line in the middle of an X symbolizes illness or death. A symmetric cross stands for the four directions of space. A diamond shape signifies water and procreative fluids. The perfectly round O represents rain water, agricultural fertility, and the tears of the Divine feminine. The chevron, or pubic V, is also the symbol of the feminine manifestation of Spirit.

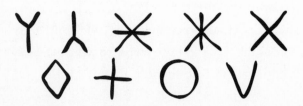

Charm Making Tools

Over time a mortar builds up a high charge of nyama from the medicines and herbs that we prepare in it. The mortar and pestle symbolize feminine and masculine principles, together representing the sacred act of creation. When we bring the mortar and pestle together, we are unifying the transcendent with the immanent. We raise our pestles high in the air, calling the heavens, and rhythmically stroke the pestle into the mortar, the womb of the earth.

One must turn the mortar on her stomach, and lay the pestle beside her, when not in use. We ritually wash our mortar and pestles with rain or well water. We do not use any other herbs or mystical potions to bathe our mortars and pestles as they are already highly charged with the nyama of the ingredients we mix in them. When one makes use of a mortar and pestle seven days in a row, they receive the necessary charge.[2] If our children lose their appetites, we give them water to drink from the mortar, the womb of the earth, that they may open their stomachs and receive nourishment.

The mortar and pestle symbolize the unification of the transcendent with the immanent, heaven with earth.

We also mix our sacrificial materials in a calabash. Though we do not eat the fruit of the calabash, the shells serve as containers for many needs in our communities, such as the storing of food and the functioning of gourds for our musical instruments. We use new, unused calabash for making powerful charms and pouring libations.

Charm Making

We always construct our charms in secret. If we want to imbue them with great amounts of power, we create them with the accompaniment of drums, invocations, and dancing. Inside the hollow of a shell or bone, or a leather pouch, we place sacred writing, mixed herbs, and any other charm ingredients. We pack them firmly into their container and often use a black resin we gather from trees to provide a solid plaster over the opening. While the resin is still soft, we may stick feathers into it, and we often add cowrie shells to the outer case.

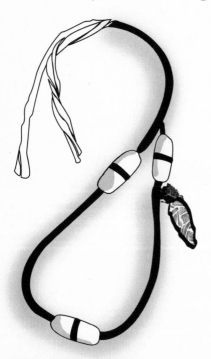

This talisman brings luck to one's business. The white cord is protection against those who may disrupt one's work or success.

We usually sew up our charms in leather cases, as these are the easiest to wear or carry. The charms we enclose in lizard skins bring prosperity to our craft. We never leave the ingredients exposed very long before we seal our charms, as the charm will lose its power. We sacrifice a chicken usually, or occasionally a larger animal for especially potent objects, and sprinkle the blood on our ingredients or on the outside of the case after it has been sewn up. We may make a number of sacrifices to it over a period of days or weeks if we want to invite a spirit to reside in it.

Upon the completion of our charm, we always spit on it; this is done to ward off disruptive spirits. Spitting is a symbolic burst of air from the mouth, imbuing the object with potent levels of nyama. We may chew up kola nuts and spit the pulp onto the ingredients or outer case. When we do not want anyone to touch a special object, we may spit on straws, and stick them all about the object. Praying and spitting over a sacred object is a means of imbuing it with one's own energy; it solidifies a prayer or incantation.

Area Charms

We place charms in various areas around the workplace or home for protection and prosperity. One may hang an amulet on a fence or from the branches of plants in a garden to prevent theft or damage. One may attach a talisman to the bow of a canoe to ensure a successful voyage. Many of us hang a charm over the doorway of the house, to bar the entrance of uninvited spirits or thieves. We often hide our charms where they will not be found.

Whenever we sell an item, we may retain a piece of the item as a charm for future endeavors. If one sells some vegetables or fruit, one may withhold a piece of the product or some leaves off the plant, after the sale, which now contain a higher level of nyama. We place these items in the garden, blessing it with abundance. If one sells a carcass, one might remove one of the small internal organs, such as the gall bladder, before handing it over to the buyer. The hunter now possesses a potent piece of seller's nyama, that he may retain for an herbal remedy or talisman to invite more success in future endeavors.

Cleansing Charms

Many of us drink or bathe with protective solutions. We boil special herbs in a pot, and then shower with the water from the mixture. The nyama of the ingredients provides a shield around our bodies and works as an effective charm. We also write sacred symbols or verses with charcoal or ink on a slate of wood or paper, and wash it off with water creating a magical solution. We make incantations and invocations, transferring the nyama of our words into the solution. A traditionalist will use sacred symbols and incantations to various spirits, while an Islamic clergy may use Islamic prayers and verses from the Koran. We will then either bathe with or drink the solution.

Portable Charms

Most of our charms we wear on our bodies around the waist, neck, ankle, or wrists. Depending on its purpose, the charm may be most effective on a certain area of the body. A hunter will wear a charm on his arm in hunting, to assure an accurate aim. A dancer may wear one about her waist to keep her fluid, and a drummer may wear a piece on his wrist to protect his hands. A charm may be worn on any part of the body to bring success in planting, fishing, buying, and selling, through the whole range of daily activities and interests.

Prayer

Prayer works like a charm, literally. We constantly offer up prayers, short mystical words, or utterances that our ancestors passed on to us. We use them on all sorts of occasions, such as when one sneezes, stumbles, or experiences fear. Essentially, we say "Blessings," or pray "that Spirit grant you a long life ..." When we send off a loved one or guest, or receive a gift from someone, we may hold their hand or head and offer a short prayer.

Broken Power

Exposing charms to potent levels of nyama can enhance their power. However, the personal charms of men and women become ineffective if they come into contact with one another's procreative fluids. Similarly, exposing them to high concentrations of nyama emanating from creation objects or procreative situations can render them useless. However, fecund environments, like the forge, can enhance *fertility* charms. One must not wear a charm when one is intimate, as the nyama of this act breaks its power. One must clean oneself well before wearing any piece after intimacy.

The sight of a woman's menstrual blood can break a man's charm if he is wearing it. A woman will not tend to her garden and will refrain from any activities that involve the production of crops, as she maintains high levels of nyama at this time. Menstrual blood contains a vast concentration of nyama that can break the power of almost any amulet or talisman.[3]

Stepping over a pestle or sitting on a mortar may also disempower a charm, as these objects serve as procreative masculine and feminine symbols. Stepping over either a mortar or a pestle seizes a lot of one's own nyama. If one breaks a pestle, one must immediately place it in water and take a shower with it to absorb some of the released nyama from the object.

Sitting on an instrument dissolves the power of a charm. The sight of a dead donkey can break one. Eating from the inside of a pot where we cook food is a charm breaker; this act shows a lack of proper respect for the care and preparation of food, creating disruptive nyama that can break a sacred piece.

Spirit Abodes

When we desire to communicate with a particular spirit regularly, we may create our own spirit abode. With a spirit abode, we do not have to experience spirit visitation or use divination techniques to access the divinity. We create a dwelling place for the spirit by constructing an object to which we sacrifice regularly. Our spirit abode usually takes the form of a sculpture or a mask. This is not an object for worship, but it becomes home to a spirit who serves our needs.

Sometimes we create a sacred object as a sanctuary for an ancestral spirit. Other times our ancestors identify a spirit who has been helpful to the family, and who will continue to serve as an intermediary for the spirit world. Our spirit abodes sometimes house our village animal spirit. We may pass on our spirit abodes for many generations, and we will also at times re-place them. Spirit abodes serve to focus our attention on the spirit world and enhance our relationship to Spirit.

Often, we only access our spirit abodes at certain times of the year to honor specific divinities or ancestors. We employ our spirit dwellings in ceremonies for fertility rites, curing sick-ness, or funerals. We perform with them on festive occasions or we invoke them during our initiation society gatherings. We utilize these sacred pieces as protective devices for certain activities or occupations.

The creation of a spirit abode is a ritual process, and usually only a smith or some specialist possesses the precise knowledge and energy to successfully construct it. The construction of this sacred object can last over a month, and during this time the carver will observe strict taboos and regularly sacrifice to the spirits. The carver must gather the object's ingredients and hunt for the most suitable animal components. The specialist pre-pares them following a series of recipes. Knowledge of the vari-ous ingredients that make up the composition of a spirit abode is necessary to create a successful dwelling for the spirit.

Like our charms, spirit abode ingredients may include ani-mal bones, vegetable matter, shells, beads, and pieces of metal. The ancestral objects contain mud, feathers, cotton, and other materials over which we make blood sacrifices. Sometimes our spirit abodes consist of riverbed stones from the dwelling places of water spirits. One may add red and white clays, medicinal plant substances, or animal horns and skins to the object.[4] We often include bird feathers or skulls in our sacred creations as an expression of their oracular powers. We may cover them with porcupine quills, signifying the preservation of knowledge and the wisdom of this animal. The quills also represent weaponry such as darts and arrows that our hunters use. These symbols on a spirit abode reveal the object's power to combat harmful spirits and behaviors within the community. Combined, all of these ingredients contain potent levels of nyama.

We compound these ingredients in secret, while drumming, dancing, and singing for the spirit. Our sacred objects must receive libations and sacrifices performed by a specialist, to invoke the power of the spirit. Rituals for a spirit abode will often occur in the evening, conducted by members of secret societies. After these elaborate ceremonies, including anointing the figure with clays, tree sap, blood, or spit, we believe the spirit abode will contain great amounts of power. The surface of the objects is often hard and thick with coatings of sacrificial materials that may include the blood of chickens or goats, chewed kola nuts, alcoholic beverages, and millet.

Many of our spirit abodes take the form of an animal such as a hippopotamus or a cow. A powerful dwelling may contain several kinds of animal representations at once. The abode may have the horns of an antelope, the body of a snake, and the mouth of a crocodile. We believe that the object possesses different traits of the various animals. Other abodes represent human beings. Sometimes we construct sculptures that resemble our past village elders, relatives, or friends. Often the form is not recognizable, except to the initiates themselves. The mysterious form warns people of its great power and keeps them away. Spirit abodes come in a variety of forms, but all of them represent incarnations of spirits.

For our initiation associations, we construct our spirit dwellings in the form of masks. A spirit will call an initiate into leadership of a secret society, who will then create or inherit a spirit abode invested with power. The object will harbor huge quantities of nyama, which the association leader and members help to activate to serve special functions for the community. The formulas for activating the sacred piece are known only to people in the secret societies. During secret society meetings, a leader may perform dances while wearing the mask. These dances respond to petitions from the community for various kinds of help, ranging from divining the cause of a family's crop failure to correcting a problem of infertility. In order to divine while dancing, the performer concentrates on combining his or her own nyama with the nyama of the spirit. Answers to the community challenges will come to the leader, and during a performance the leader will reveal them to the audience.

A spirit abode often remains in a hidden location when not in use at a ceremony. We continue to offer it incantations, water, porridge, and blood sacrifice from a chicken, goat, or cow. A spirit abode will not come alive without sacrifice, but one that receives many sacrifices can become quite dangerous. We make an object ineffective by not offering sacrifice to it. Sometimes we call an ineffective piece "dead," because the spirit no longer resides in it. If we want to bring a spirit abode alive again, we will restore its power through rituals and sacrifice.

5
HERBS & HEALING RECIPES

The giant tree grows from a grain.

We rely upon thousands of plants to serve our needs. We drink concoctions of herbs, inhale their steam, shower with them, and apply them externally. We burn herbs and inhale the smoke for medicine and protection. We boil mixtures and bathe with the tea. We extract the juices, saps, or resins, and apply them to our bodies. We place them in bundles and mix them with other ingredients for amulets and talismans. We make use of every part of a plant; the seeds, leaves, flowers, and roots. We always imbue our herbal remedies with prayer and incantations, which strengthen their ability to heal.

Baobab Tree

Of all our plants, the sacred baobab tree (*Adansonia digitata*) provides us with the most blessings. The baobab supplies us with food, water, clothing, shelter, medicine, tools, and cosmetics. We use the fibers from the bark to make rope, mats, baskets, musical instrument strings, paper, and cloth. We maintain strong prohibitions against defacing or cutting down this special tree.

The baobab sprouts large white flowers that open at night to produce great amounts of nectar. We soak the fruit of the baobab in water to make a tasty drink. Consuming the fruit can help to reduce a fever and remedy diarrhea. We place the shells of the baobab fruit around our homes to keep the geckos away.

We boil the leaves and make sauces we add to our meals, which can treat fever and general fatigue. We also consume the leaves to effectively treat more serious ailments such as asthma, kidney and bladder diseases, worm infestations, and internal pains. The leaves serve as a tonic, a blood cleanser, and a general sanitizer. We also boil the leaves and make a liquid solution to consume for sedation, colic, ear trouble, and tumors. We make ointments and lotions from the leaves for insect bites, inflammations, aches, and wounds.

We roast and crush the seeds of the fruits to a paste, which we apply to our teeth and gums for aches or infections. Eating the seeds is also a helpful remedy for diarrhea. We extract oil from the seeds to relieve aches, pains, rheumatism, and serious skin conditions. We believe if we drink water in which a baobab's seeds have been soaked we will receive a form of protection.

The bark contains a gum we use for cleaning sores and making a mouthwash for toothaches. We boil the bark and make a drink to reduce fevers and to prevent the return of malaria. We make salt and soaps from the bark ash. Some of us pulverize the roots to make a red paste we apply to the skin as make-up or a skin-moisturizer. We also grind the roots into a dry powder which we rinse with for toothaches, or consume as a medicine for malaria.

The trunk of the baobab stores a great amount of water, which we draw from in times of drought. Our shamans often hide their charms and spirit abodes here to imbue them with more power. Many of our shamans have been buried in the trunk of a baobab. We sometimes soak the bark of the baobab in water and wash our newborns in it. Like the tree, our children grow with great strength and power. We make offerings at the base of the tree for fertility, a fine harvest, and prosperity. We believe this special tree stores high concentrations of nyama and is home to many spirits.

Jala

Jala (*Khaya senegalensis*) is a common herb we drink for an intestinal cleansing and to boost energy. We soak the bark in water and we drink the soup to bring down fevers and to alleviate constipation. We often drink this medicine to combat general fatigue, as well. We often tie a twig of the jala plant around the waists of our newborns for the first week of their lives, to protect them from harmful forces and spirits. Adults also bathe with this herb to ward off illness and misfortune.

Kolobé

Many of us drink kolobé or kinkéliba (*Combretum micranthum*) tea daily for general well-being. We often consume this tea to bring down fevers or to treat colds, flu viruses, aches, and pains. Kolobé is a natural diuretic and helps to speed up the healing process when one is ill. We drink kolobé to lower blood pressure and to prevent malaria. We combine this plant with other herbs to treat infections, and we apply solutions of the leaves or the roots to speed up the healing of old wounds. This herb serves as an antibacterial and antispasmodic as well.

Kola Nuts

We make use of kola nuts almost daily in our homes and communities. Kola nuts serve as our medicine, offerings, gifts, and divination. We consume kola nuts to treat boils, shingles, stomach problems, and impotency. Kola, which contains high levels of caffeine, is a stimulant. Many among us who do not consume alcohol or smoke tobacco may eat kola nuts to give us energy.

We offer kola nuts to our ancestors, nature spirits, and one another. We give them away at all of our ceremonies. Acceptance of a gift of kola communicates trust and connection. We exchange them with loved ones to strengthen our bonds. If one eats a kola nut and then tells a lie, one may fall very ill.

Mandesunsun

We use mandesunsun (*Annona senegalensis*) both externally and internally. We apply the crushed leaves to wasp stings. We boil the herb in water and apply it to arthritic joints. We pulverize the leaves and bark and mix it with shea butter for a healing ointment. A woman will pulverize the roots and mix it with peanut sauce to consume during pregnancy. She will also either bathe in it or drink it when she has pregnancy complications such as edema. We mix mandesunsun with other herbs and recipes to treat impotence and mental illnesses.

Neem

Neem (*Azadirachta indica*) is a special plant of which we also utilize every part.[1] It is an antibacterial, antiviral, antiseptic herb that strengthens our immune systems. We extract the juice from the leaves and roots of neem and apply it externally to treat wounds, burns, sprains, bruises, rheumatism, fungal infections, yeast infections, gum and tooth disease, and earaches. We make an ointment from the pulp to destroy lice and treat other skin diseases. We boil the leaves of this herb and consume the tea for headaches, fever, fatigue, allergies, sore throats, colds, flu viruses, digestive problems, and food poisoning. We consume the oil from the nuts for cramps and ulcers.

Many believe neem can help to cure the most serious diseases, including diabetes, cancer, and immune deficiencies. Some of us consume this plant for hepatitis, sexually transmitted diseases, blood disorders, heart disease, kidney problems, nerve disorders, and malaria. In large doses neem is slightly narcotic. One must not use this herb for more than two weeks at a time. For chronic disorders, one must refrain from consuming this medicine for at least a week after taking it for a two-week period.

Ntomi

Ntomi (*Tamarindus indica*) has numerous herbal uses. We drink ntomi (tamarind juice) for constipation, ulcers, and illnesses caused by flatworms of the bladder or intestinal tract. We use the pulp of the fruit to make a drink for reducing fevers and treating sore throats. We also consume the leaves for jaundice, and drink a solution of the bark for asthma.

We soak in an herbal bath of ntomi for sore muscles, and rinse our eyes with it for itching and pain. We mix the herb with honey and goat's milk, and apply it to wounds to prevent scarring. We pulverize the bark into a powder, add salt, and mix it in a special meat soup for impotence.

Ntoro

Ntoro (*Ficus capensis*) is a remedy for many ailments, especially arthritis. We tie a handful of the leaves of ntoro into a bundle and simmer it in water. We rub the packet over our joints. We mix the bark and fruit with a porridge made from millet or couscous and eat it for infertility. We also crush the unripe fruit and mix it with mandesunsun into a powder that we consume daily for infertility. We boil the roots of ntoro with other plants to drink during pregnancy.

Roselle

Roselle (*Hibiscus sabdariffa*) is a popular food beverage and medicine. We serve this special herbal drink at many of our ceremonies. We also drink roselle medicinally for indigestion and loss of appetite. We consume roselle as a remedy for colds, respiratory inflammation, circulation disorders, water retention, urinary infections, and constipation. We crush the leaves and consume them to treat cramps and reduce blood pressure. We make a lotion with the leaves for sores and wounds. We apply heated leaves to cracks in the feet and on boils and ulcers for healing.

Shea Butter

Shea butter is both a food and a healing product for us. Shea butter comes from the nut of an edible, sweet fruit that we eat. We also cook with shea oil. Women usually make the shea butter in the rainy seasons from May to August when we harvest the shea nut fruits. The sweet fruit ripens right before the rains, and we gather the nuts to dry. We heat up the nuts until the outer shell breaks and mix water with the remaining substance, which we cook many times over, until it is the right consistency. Making shea butter is a long and challenging process, which we hold sacred.

We apply shea butter as a skin moisturizer, for aging skin, and for skin ailments. We massage the butter into the skin to relax the muscles and to treat sprains, wounds, and colds. We apply it as an aftershave, a hair balm for dry and brittle hair, and on the umbilical cord of newborn babies to ensure healing. Our musicians use the butter for the skins of drums to prevent their drying and cracking. We apply shea butter to our heads for soothing, cooling, and spiritual cleanses.

We sometimes burn shea butter in our oil lamps for ritual purposes. We burn the butter in a sculpted object that symbolizes a particular spirit. We invoke the divinity by illuminating the lamp with the burning of this sacred oil.

Body Remedies

To cure a headache, we sometimes recite an incantation over a cotton string, tie a knot, and spit on it. We make three or seven knots. We usually tie three knots for headaches, neckaches, footaches, and wristaches, and seven knots for backaches. We then wear the blessed amulet over the pained area. We save these healing charms for a later time when we can use them again. We may tie seven knots together with red, white, and black cotton string to ward away harmful spirits. We tie up one or two of the ends together when we are in the home, or we attach all of the ends together when we leave for the day.

We also employ a special natural remedy by drawing dead blood to heal certain kinds of headaches, swollen bruises, or sore backs. We take one shot glass, light a match, and throw it inside the glass. We immediately put the cup up to the skin. We then take a razor and make a small cut to let a little of the blood drain. For cleaning the incision, we gather the soot from our tree leaves that catch the smoke from our cooking pots, and use this dark powder as a disinfectant.

6
WILDLIFE &
ELEMENTS

No matter how long the wood floats in the
river, it can never be a crocodile.

Wildlife

Everything that has life speaks; everything that speaks tells the story of Spirit. This is the language of our ancestors, the language that teaches us how to live in harmony with our surroundings and with one another. Many of us have lost this language, though everything around us continues to speak. When we listen carefully to the whistle of the wind and the cries of the bush, we hear this language. When we observe closely the blossoms of the earth and the colors of the seasons, we connect to this sacred language that brings us closer to Spirit.

Ants

Ants come to our homes to pick up sacrifice for the spirits. A visit from an army of ants is a blessing; it is an obvious sign from the spirits that we need to make an offering. One may also leave an offering inside an anthill.

Bees

Beehives near our homes bring blessings, and serve to ward away illness. We say that if one is stung by a bee, one may live a long life. One must also be careful around bees, as mystical practitioners sometimes make use of them to transport their potions to others.

Birds

Birds communicate knowledge between humans and divinities. These magical creatures mediate between us and the heavens, and make available to us the wisdom of Spirit. Pigeons are the most informative of the birds. Sometimes they will cry three different cries to let us know if someone we love crosses over. They will also utter three cries, three days in advance, to foretell the coming of a visitor. The swallow is water spirit's airborne messenger.

Buffalo

Buffaloes possess unique powers. If a buffalo stares a hunter in the eyes before it is shot, the gun can reverse and kill the hunter. We boil buffalo or cow feet in water to make a soup that helps to purify the blood and improve energy.

Chameleons

Chameleons are highly mystical creatures with great capacities. The chameleon adapts to its environment, and takes on the color of its surroundings. We say there are three teeth of the chameleon; one tooth that is deadly, one that can make one poor all of one's life, and the other that can make one rich. These represent the many shades of the chameleon. We make use of chameleons in our charms to disguise us or make ourselves invisible.

Cows

Cows are special animals that we often sacrifice for important occasions, such as marriages or funerals. We use cow hides for our instruments. Cow urine is a potent substance we combine with other herbal treatments to cleanse those with mental disturbances.

Crocodiles

Crocodiles are powerful agents of mystical forces and energy. Crocodiles sometimes serve as mouthpieces for diviners. The jaws of a crocodile symbolize this reptile's ability to consume harmful energy and mystical practices. The crocodile is one of the water spirit's representatives, and guards the waters from disruptive animals and people. It also collects sacrifices for the spirit of water.

Deer

Deer are mysterious, though gentle, animals. We do not kill the deer if it stands on its hind legs. This may mean it is pregnant or has a baby to feed. Killing a pregnant deer can bring death to a family within a year. We use deer horns for business success. The horn is a great symbol of the bush and serves as a container for our medicines and a decoration for our spirit abodes.

Dogs and Cats

Dogs and cats are not usually pets for us. Dogs see spirits and may scare them off when they bark. Protective divinities may shy away from a home with a dog. Cats carry high levels of nyama that exacts great revenge on those who harm them; mystical practitioners make use of these animals for various activities. Rabbits, sheep, goats, and chickens are our pets; they absorb sickness and harm from our home.

This mask representing an elephant emphasizes the creature's most distinctive attributes.

Elephants

Elephants are big, strong, intelligent animals full of nyama and dangerous to harm. The large size of elephant ears represents their powers of inner hearing. Elephant excrement is especially potent. Sometimes we bathe a newborn with it so the child will possess the powerful qualities of the elephant.

Gazelles

Gazelles are artful and cunning, the source of their mischief residing in their livers. We use gazelle parts for our amulets and talismans. The nyama of this animal imbues the charm with the qualities of its craftiness.

Goats

Goats bring us many blessings. They provide sacrifice for our ceremonies, meat for our nourishment, and skins for our drums. They absorb our illnesses and troubles. We sometimes feed them beer when they are ill.

Hyenas

Hyenas are powerful animals. Our children believe that they are foolish animals; our elders know they are cunning creatures. One must never eat a hyena; they are full of poisons, which we place inside some of our talismans and protective charms. The hyena's intestines are especially toxic and even a taste of them can bring death. We wrap many of our amulets with their skins to bring success in business. We give the tail of a hyena, covered with special ingredients, to those who cross over when away from their village, to help them to return home for their burial. Sometimes we use its head for special powers.

The red hyena is the most impressive of its kind. If one shoots this hyena and it jumps in the air, lands on its mouth, and screams three times, each year someone in the family will die. The hyena is shrewd and has the power to make itself invisible. Using hyena parts for our charms charges them with these qualities.

Lions

Lions are extraordinary creatures that we avoid killing. If salt touches a lion's body within one's home, the inhabitants of the house risk death. Such an act symbolizes that the meat is being prepped for consumption; any hint at attempting to kill and eat the lion signals trouble.

Lizards

Lizards often symbolize fertility and prosperity. The water iguana is one of the representatives of the spirit of water. The symbol of a water lizard engraved on a house protects it from thieves. Sometimes we hang the head above the door to the entrance of our home. The small gray gecko can be quite dangerous, and is a symbol of harmful mystical practices.

Owls

Owls are mystical birds that often carry messages for us about death and war. They send word of those who have crossed over, and warnings to opposing warriors in times of battle.

Panthers

Panthers are symbols of the Divine feminine. Soliwulén is a red panther that is in charge of protecting young boys and girls in the days before their adult initiation.

Porcupines

Porcupines are wise animals. We attach porcupine parts to some of our spirit abodes to represent their preservation of wisdom. The quills also portray a form of weaponry and reveal the object's power to combat disruptive spirits and behaviors. We sometimes braid hair using porcupine spines.

Rabbits

Rabbits, or any other long-eared animals, hear every sound and so we often display images of them on our homes to protect our property from uninvited guests. The rabbit is also a clever creature that often outwits the larger animals of the bush, and appears as a jester in many of our stories.

Snakes

Snakes possess tremendous concentrations of nyama. Any snake may represent an ancestor. We wear the bones of serpents around the waist as a cure for backaches.

Slithering between the earth and the heavens, the python is an especially mystical snake. Many among us believe the python's head symbolizes Spirit. This snake is a potent symbol of fertility.

The cobra's spit is blinding if it hits the back of one's head. We do not kill a standing cobra, as our children may die at the same height of the cobra when it is killed. One must avoid the bite of the earth-colored camouflage snake, as this may cause any healed wounds on the body to bleed.

The boa constrictor flies every year from village to village. If a mortar is left upturned, it will catch the flying boa like a vacuum. This is one reason we always leave our mortars face down when we are not using them. A pregnant woman who passes a dead boa will cause it to move. If she eats the snake, her children may be strong. We use the fat of the boa to place inside the ear to heal earaches.

One must never touch the snake with the short little tail as it may bring death. This noble snake will kill if it smells human excrement. The white snake bites only the youngest in a family.

Toads

Toads are exceptional reptiles with the ability to transform themselves into other creatures; they are often aids for mystical practitioners.

Tortoises

Tortoises are creatures of both the land and water; they represent feminine power and are a part of many of our fertility rituals. The tortoise is often a trickster in our tales, being able to appear and disappear, though it is sometimes outwitted. The protective tortoise shell guards against the harmful mystical practices of others. We use the bones from the legs of tortoises as anklets, in order to give us the tortoise's qualities of endurance. Some among us may also wear the jawbone of this reptile around the neck as a preventive charm against toothaches.

Vultures

Vultures are noble birds with big hearts that do not kill their prey. They shed their feathers every hundred years to be reborn. The vulture is the bird of the sky, who sometimes delivers our offerings to the spirits. We place bird feathers on our powerful spirit abodes to imbue them with the wisdom of these creatures.

Many of the smaller and more vulnerable creatures of the bush often possess remarkable intelligence and unique abilities. We learn at an early age which animals contain especially high levels of nyama and will exact revenge on those of us who harm them. We do not kill the lion, tiger, leopard, red hyena, elephant, or crocodile. Only hunters attempt to kill these animals at times to increase their own levels of energy and power. We may mix the urine and feces of these creatures with herbal remedies for curing mental illness, applying the solution to a shaved head or over the entire body of an individual who is ill.

In the sacred wilderness of creatures, spirits, healing, knowledge, and power, every form of life represents some divine quality of Spirit. Animals and wildlife are some of the most powerful communicators for the realm of Spirit. In Africa, it is very difficult to hide anything from anyone as "The Message of the Bird" story and song teaches us.

The Message of the Bird

One day, there was a big celebration in the village. Everyone was dancing, drumming, and singing, while next door in a little house by the party, an old woman took her last breath. When her son saw that his mother had passed on, he decided not to announce it to the community, as he did not want to disturb the festivities. An hour later a bird flew to a high branch in the big bana tree (*Ceiba pentandra*) and began to sing. The bird came to announce to the gathering at the party that their beloved elder had made her transition onto the realm of the ancestors. The bird with the message sang three times. A bard heard the bird and sang its message to the crowd of people:

> *One bird is sitting on a branch in the big bana tree crying,*
> *Bird, don't cry*
> *Somebody is hiding a departed spirit*
> *but an empty room cannot hide.*

Elements

The four essential elements—air, fire, water, and earth—are some of the most basic forms of Divine manifestation and serve as important intermediaries between us and Spirit. Droughts, floods, and other natural deviations all serve as communication from the divinities that we do not have harmony or peace in our communities. We always perform rites to restore the balance of the natural order and appease the spirits.

Air

In the beginning, out of vibration a whirlwind of activity flourished. The spirit of air is mystery, energy, activity, and desire. We honor the spirit of air for the life it gives us. Air communicates to us through temperature and movement. Any extremes in temperature or any strong movement of air are messages from the spirit world.[1] If the air twirls in a circle when it is hot, it is often a disruptive spirit. We sometimes point our right little finger at a swirling body of air for it to depart peacefully. A tornado is a neglected spirit retrieving possessions from us. A gust of wind will often follow communication with a spirit or ancestor who is acknowledging a prayer or offering.

Air has a special connection with the other elements as it is an inspiration for their movements and transitions. Gusts of wind extinguish fires, stir up sandstorms, and spur on swells of waves. Air is integral to shaping, molding, and fueling the other elements at will.

Fire

The spirit of fire, closely allied to air, is inspiration, animation, enthusiasm, transformation, and courage. We revere the power of fire, which is often a symbol in our rituals for transition, endurance and change. When we experience our rites of passage into adulthood, we befriend the spirit of fire. Fire eating, walking, and jumping are often a part of our rituals that reveal our ability to overcome obstacles and challenges.

In our communities, that which is hot or heated refers to power and aggression. We speak of those among us with vast amounts of nyamic power as possessing great heat. Among this group, blacksmiths are masters of fire, and have the ability to transform, ignite, incite, and create. These powerful practitioners transform the sacred substance of iron with fire to create tools and ritual objects. All that we rely upon for our daily use and worship comes to us through the dynamic spirit of fire.

Water

Water was born of a bubble of Spirit's saliva, as Spirit uttered the words of creation.[2] The spirit of water symbolizes equilibrium; it tempers the activities of air and fire. Water reflects the sky and everything between; we say, then, that the spirit of water is the reflector, the great balancer, and the container of shadow and light. Rain, rainbows, thunder, and lightning are signs that we heed or utilize when we communicate with the spirit of water.[3]

When one accidentally spills water, we read this as a sign of peace and dip our fingers into it to anoint our face and head with. When we accidentally spill hot water, we pour cool water over it immediately to neutralize the burn to the earth, and the disruptive message it sends.

Whenever we depart on a journey, we pour water at our doorway and pray for protection and safety. We sometimes spill water on the ground before we leave for an important meeting or event, or we pour water in front of our homes after a disturbed or blessed dream. Sleeping near a glass of water invites pleasant dreams. We often leave a bucket of water outside for the day, to be heated by the sun and receive potent nyama from the heavens. In the evening we take a shower with this energized water, which offers us special protection and makes clear obscure dreams that may have visited us the night before. We always take a blessed shower with the first rain.

Washing with water is also the most common way we purify ourselves or an area for our rituals and rites of passage. Ritual bathing not only removes physical dirt, but it washes away undesirable habits and patterns. Purifying oneself or one's space with water opens the way for inner purification. We wash away layers that block us from our true selves. Washing is an important part of our rituals for our children entering into adulthood and couples entering marriage. Shamans wash themselves before prayer, ritual activities, and charm making. We do not bathe on Monday mornings, so that we begin our week with a potent level of nyama. We never wash when the sun is especially hot, or when it is setting, as spirits are active during these times.

We always serve water to the spirits of our ancestors before posing questions or making requests. We always serve water to our guests when they enter our homes, whether they are thirsty or not. To refuse to drink the water is to refuse the people who offer it. We wait to address our visitors until they have a drink of water.

The ocean is home to the mighty spirit of water. Some oceans do not like strangers and will swallow them with the tide. The oceans fish for people as people fish in the ocean. Those of us who live near the ocean make a yearly sacrifice. We also bathe in the ocean to purify ourselves and for protection from harmful spirits. One can take a ritual bath seven Fridays in a row, in the ocean water, for protection. When one washes in the ocean, one must first clean the face three times, then the body three times and offer up a prayer. We often make our sacrifices to the spirit of water at night when the tides are calm.

Whenever we make contact with a body of water for the first time (usually with a river or lake), we always say or sing the following short prayer to show our reverence to the spirit of water:

> *The river bank, I want to wash my face by the river bank*
> *The river bank, I want to wash my face by the river bank*
> *The river bank, I want to wash my face by the river bank*
> *To wash with the river water is sacred.*

Earth

The earth is Spirit incarnate, teaching us how to live, grow, and die. Earth represents durability, stability, and permanence. The spirit of earth teaches us patience, perseverance, and resolution. The giver of life, earth inspires our deep reverence. When we invoke spirits, we pay homage first to the earth. We make sacrifices to the mother of all beings, as the productivity of the entire planet depends upon her.[4] A farmer will not open the earth without performing incantation, nor plant a seed before blessing it. Planting is an act of creation; it is usually the men among us who break the ground, and the women who bury the seeds in the womb of the earth. We conduct rituals from planting to harvest. We take what is essential for survival; anything more is sacrilege.

We derive many of our customs and prohibitions from the land; we base them on our respect for her. If food spills on the ground, our ancestors are calling for sacrifice. We are careful to not spill millet on the ground, as millet is an important grain on which we depend. Cayenne or black pepper spilled on the ground is a sign of disharmony in the household. We must pick it up and spill water on it to cool off the fire. We will not relieve ourselves without first excusing ourselves to the spirits of the earth, so they may move away from the spot that we will soil. We never swear and curse the ground, nor are we intimate on the bare ground. We maintain the cleanliness and sanctity of the earth, which will one day enclose us in her womb.

7
DREAMS, SIGNS
& SYMBOLS

*A hippopotamus can be made
invisible in dark water.*

The symbol for us is not abstract, it is an echo of
the spirit world. We receive our knowledge of life
from our sacred oral traditions that interpret these
symbols for us. As energy and spirits inhabit everything around us, we are careful to study their representations and behavior. We observe the movement of energy, the cycles of nature, and the patterns of the universe. We honor the prohibitions
and customs that govern our relations with the sur-
rounding forces. We are thoughtful about our own
actions, gestures, and words and the deeper messages they convey.

We recognize that all interactions are meaningful. This awareness serves to keep us present, alert,
and open. Our openness fosters dialogue with the

spirits. Observing the signs and symbols teaches us about the divine and mystical nature of the universe and our special role in it.

We are sensitive to the conditions of harmony and peace around us. Disharmony is a powerful sign from the realm of Spirit that we heed seriously. We realize that we each contribute to the balance and serenity of the forces of nature through our conduct. The various signs and symbols of the universe keep us aware of how well we are maintaining our equilibrium with the forces of life.

As well, we believe in an inherent balance in all things. All that is visible corresponds to an invisible source. Everything around us contains light and shadow, something easy to perceive and something not. All of creation holds equally feminine and masculine principles. The shapes of objects reveal to us the meaning of their symbols. That which is hollow is often a reflection of femininity, while the projecting part of an object often represents masculinity.

We do not have to read too closely to perceive the messages around us. We interpret physical signs literally and this tells us many things about the activities of the spirits. We reflect on the symbols everywhere and leave nothing to chance.

Dreams

Many times, the spirits speak with us through our dreams. A few of us can see things in our dreams, exactly as they will happen, but most of us cannot. When we dream, we often see the opposite of what will transpire.[1] Dreams of having money may forewarn of financial challenges ahead. Dreams of tears and pain can indicate great happiness awaiting. Dreams of ceremonies, parties, and festivities are unfavorable. Dreams of blood or accidents foretell of peace, and dreams about death may reveal a long life.

Dreams of water, climbing a tree, or flying high in the air all indicate blessings and longevity. Dipping one's head in the ocean is a sign of money to come. Dreaming of the rain is auspicious. If a tooth falls out, this is a sign of impending fortune. Rocks and umbrellas are also symbols of money. Dead fish are warnings of illness and misfortune. Eggs or peanuts can be signs of betrayal. Dreams of the police, military, or those in uniform forewarn of struggle in the future. Dreams of snakes reveal a future pregnancy. If the snake bites the back, it will be a boy; if it bites the front of the body, it will be a girl.

Body Signs

The nyama of a thought or experience manifests through signs in the body, including itching, twitching, or aching. When the right foot itches, new shoes are on the way. When the left foot itches, travel plans are near. The right hand that itches will spend money in the days ahead. The left hand that itches will receive money. Itching inside of the hand foretells that these events will occur soon; itching outside of the middle of the hand reveals it will not happen immediately.

The right eye that flutters will see something or someone from the past. The left eye that flutters will see something unpleasant, or something it has not seen before. We place a small piece of wood, such as a splinter, on the eyelash and blink a couple times to protect us from seeing what we do not wish to see. An itching or twitching right ear will hear something favorable, and an itching or twitching left one will hear that which it does not want to hear. A nose that twitches warns of an acquaintance or loved one experiencing hardship or death. A twitching right cheek foretells of troubles subsiding, while on a left cheek it cautions of false blame or accusations.

Illnesses often relate to harm done to the essence of a body part. If one sees something one should not have, one may develop an eye infection. If one hears things one should not have, one may develop an earache. If one absorbs or takes on something one should not have, one may develop a stomachache.

To see an old person naked is forbidden. If this happens, one must quickly turn away and leave immediately. If one sees an elder naked and quickly bows the head down in shame, a headache is sure to visit. We call this a shame headache, which is similar to the kind that may visit during hot weather. We make a little cut on each side of the head or inside the nostrils to allow a little blood to run and relieve the pain. The incision allows for the concentrations of nyama to escape and helps to balance the energy in that region of the body.

When a pregnant woman is hungry but does not receive food from those who are eating in her presence, we say her swallowed spit burns the child inside of her, discoloring the baby's skin. One must always offer food to a pregnant woman.

The young among us who begin to bald before their time are often those who see things; they are those older than their years. Those whose baldness quickly makes a path to the nape of the neck may soon join the realm of the ancestors. A bearded woman among us is a powerful woman and will wear her beard to yield her influence.

Signs of Action

The regular use of the left hand is not common among us and therefore contains special levels of nyama. We usually use only our right hands for eating and greetings, and our left hands for bathroom activities. When we make a long journey, we will depart from our friends and families by shaking with our left hands. One who puts something away with the left hand risks losing it. A left-handed woman who washes a soldier's clothes before battle will help to bring him protection from death. When we clear a field for planting, we begin the first three cuts of grass with the left hand, to remove the high levels of nyama from the earth.

When we want to ensure that any meal or beverage we are about to consume will not poison us, we place a left little finger inside any part of the food or drink and flick a piece or drop into the air. This provides a seal of protection from any potential harm. If we want to remember something we are being told, we tell it to our left little finger and the information will be available for us to access at any time. Deliberately pointing either little finger at someone is a hostile act, and is intended to drain their mystical powers.

If we do not want someone to remember something we are conveying to them, we place our right toe into the ground as we relay the information. The big toe represents one's guardian spirit; if one stubs it before venturing out of the house it is a warning from the spirits to take extra care.

We stay indoors when the sun is hot overhead or when it is setting. Village elders will not sit and meet during these times when spirits are especially active. We do not call out to one another and attract unwanted attention or spirits. We send others to relay our messages.

We do not talk of things we have; this is presumptuous. We do not count our children or say the number of them aloud. Instead, if someone asks, we may say we have five "calabash spoons" or five "pieces of wood." Nor do we count money or things of value aloud as the spirits may desire to have them for themselves.

Travel Signs

We begin any journey with a lot of preparation. Equipping oneself with the proper protective pieces is more important than bringing along enough food or clothing. We first divine what dangers may await; diviners will tell us what sacrifice to make before we depart. We then make the appropriate sacrifices and secure the necessary charms, which can take up to a month to create.

When we exit from our homes, we pour water at the door and step over it, to ensure a peaceful journey. One must not step back into the home after performing this ritual. Sometimes we also draw nine straight lines in the dirt next to our home, uttering the promise that when we return we will draw the tenth line.

The interpretation of travel signs varies greatly between villages and even among members of the same family. Men and women have their own particular signs. For many of us, if the first person one meets upon departure is a woman, particularly one with a wrapped head, this is a favorable sign. To sight a man first forewarns of trouble.

We observe the behavior of animals around us as we set foot on our journeys. If the rooster crows during off-hours, between dusk and three in the morning, it is a sign not to travel. The sight of a rabbit can be auspicious, especially if the trip involves making money. If one is on the way to hunt or work, a hyena is not a favorable sign. If a particular animal crosses one's path from left to right this can be favorable, from right to left somewhat favorable. If the animal appears from the left and runs ahead in the direction one is traveling, this can be highly auspicious. If the animal runs in the opposite direction of one's travel, this could be a sign to cancel the trip. Some among us believe one must begin one's journey with the left foot first. If the right foot meets with an obstacle upon commencing one's journey, this could be a warning of challenges to come.

We observe the signs that may foretell of death upon a journey. The cry of an owl may warn that one among us in the community may cross over. A falling star indicates the death of a great leader or elder.

Symbols of the Celestial Bodies

We appreciate the celestial bodies as manifestations of the power of Spirit. The sun, the moon, and the stars represent the bright, reliable, and luminous aspects of Spirit. They guide us, locate us in time, and shine down on us with warmth and beauty.

The sun nurtures the earth and her creatures. We honor the sun for the life it gives us, the food it feeds us, and the warmth it brings us. The sun guides our daily activities and communicates to us when the spirits are most active. When the sun is hot overhead or setting, we refrain from many activities to avoid the roaming spirits.

The moon is the celestial body ruling femininity, sexuality, and procreation. We watch her swell like a pregnant belly, becoming full and round, and then quickly wane only to reproduce again. The moon teaches us how to gracefully develop and grow with her.

Our sacred ceremonies follow the days of the lunar month. We perform incantations for each day, each phase of the moon. The day of the new moon is a favorable time for making offerings. Those born on a bright full moon will forever be seen; they are those who may experience fame and praise, but also those who will experience scrutiny and close observation.

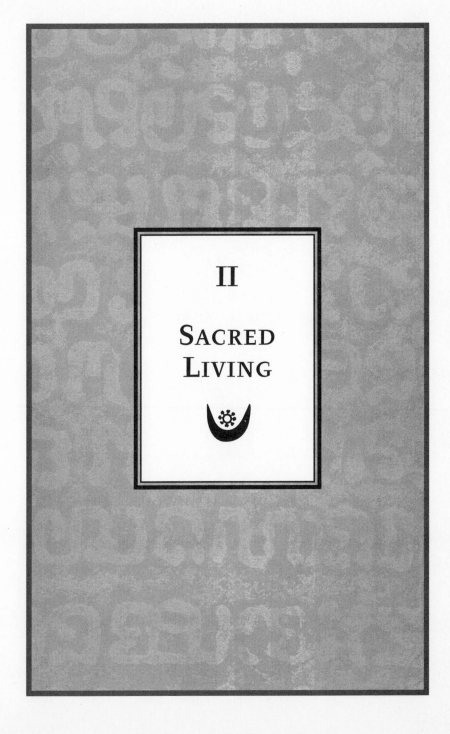

II

SACRED LIVING

8
VILLAGE LIFE

If speech constructs the village,
silence builds the world.

All space is sacred. We reserve special areas in our
environment to honor the spirits who inhabit different parts, which, together, sanctify the whole of
creation. We are mindful where we harvest, hunt,
work, and live. We make peace with the spirits
before we perform any activity or construct any
dwelling.

Our beliefs, thoughts, and behavior determine
the kind of spirits we draw into our surroundings.
We do not use law to enforce ethical behavior; we
live with the knowledge that our actions are visible
to the realm of Spirit. We understand that our ancestors are watching, and harmful conduct may have
repercussions on our family, our community, and
our environment. Disruptive acts are felt deeply by
all of us who will carry the shame for one person.

Anyone who is ill, hurt, or weak affects every one of us, and the entire community will participate in the healing. We chant, dance, drum, and make offerings and sacrifices to communicate with the spirits for their assistance. The love and support of the community alone is often enough to bring about a quick recovery. We value generosity and acts of selflessness, which are essential to the well-being of our environment. Each person has a place in our communities. Everyone is needed, valued, and appreciated.

Village Elders

We hold in high esteem those who come before us and possess more experience and wisdom; these are our elders. Our elders are fluent in the language of our ancestors and impart to us the knowledge on how to live and worship. They teach us all of the prohibitions, violations, and remedies for our communities. They are masters of ritual, rituals that will communicate to the spirits. Elders are our negotiators, moderators and counselors.

We always greet our elders. To ignore an elder is a sign of great disrespect. If one passes an elder who is carrying or transporting something, one must offer help. We always relieve them of their loads. We do not look our elders directly in their eyes, but keep our heads bowed as a sign of respect.

When we sit before our elders, we sit at a distance to give them their space and show our reverence. We also take off our shoes in their presence. We do not remove our hats, but we always remove our shoes to sanctify the area and keep it clean. We tread lightly around them and stay connected to the earth.

When we make inquiries of our elders, we present ourselves modestly and in gratitude. We do not address our elders with excitement and curiosity. We approach them respectfully, quietly, and sincerely. We do not show our elders what we know, only what we do not know. We listen to their counsel without interruption. We save our questions and our expressions of appreciation until the end of their teachings.

Village Living: The connectedness of all things.
(Drawing by Naomi Doumbia)

The ritual of speaking in reverence to our elders preserves and maintains the sacredness of the wisdom they impart. We express our respect for the knowledge itself, the power that it holds. We reveal our appreciation for the containers of that wisdom. Knowledge is communication from the realm of the spirit on how to live, how to grow, and how to be. Knowledge becomes information when it loses its sacred character. Knowledge that becomes only information is dangerous. Gossip, flattery, and deceit can be the results of the reckless sharing of information.

Often our elders will claim not to know what we ask of them. We must have patience for their answers, which will not always come at the time that we want. Our elders test our worthiness of receiving the wisdom we seek. They test our readiness to receive their teachings. They ensure that we are prepared to use the knowledge they impart to us wisely. Elders will never reveal everything at once.

When our elders do speak, they teach us through symbol and story. They teach us the hidden meaning of things. They hear what we cannot hear, and see what we cannot see. They speak about knowledge that we cannot obtain on our own. Our elders speak from the realm of our ancestors, a place to which they are deeply connected and where they will soon return. The stories from our elders describe the origins of our communities, and the ways for living with integrity and peace within them. Our elders teach us how to live in harmony with everything: in our relationships, in nature and in Spirit.

Sacred Space

In most villages, we have two gates. The west gate of the village is the gate of daily departure and entry. The east gate is the gate for our ancestors, for those who leave or return from a journey, and for the passage of our funeral processions. We make sacrifices at the east gate, and often offer kola nuts, food, and special stones or objects.

Before we enter the west gate into any village, we say a short prayer to bless our entrance. As visitors to a village, we may offer gifts of tobacco or kola nuts to members of the community. As guests we will always be served water to drink, of which we will partake to solidify our bond with our host.

We reserve the middle of the village for our ceremonial temple. We may construct a round dome, with doors opening to each of the four directions. No one must enter this dwelling, which we save for our community prayers and rituals. To secure the center of our village as sacred space is to communicate that the sacred is the center of our lives. It is our focal point, from which everything emanates and upon which we all depend.

In all villages, we secure a meeting place for our elders. Every community decision comes from them at this sacred area under a tree. This space is not for any other use. Children must not play here, and adults will not work here. Planning for marriages, rituals, burials, and ceremonies take place at the meeting ground of our elders.

Sacred Water

Every community preserves a special place for sacred water. We may reserve a well, a pond, or a stream as an area that we will not use. We save this water until there may be a drought in the village. We sacrifice this area to the spirit of water, and keep aware of our dependence on this sacred substance. One must not mix this water with any other water. Some villages may conduct ceremonies for sacred water.

Sacred Wood

We also reserve a sacred wood in our villages. Wood is an extension of earth, and is a symbol of protection, stability, and prosperity. We use wood for our rituals, ceremonies, and music. We set aside a special place in the forest for honoring the gifts it provides us, and often encircle it with thorny branches or bushes to demarcate it. Trees, plants, and animals also make up the area of sacred wood, and we remember its blessings and many uses in our lives: the healing medicines, food, shelter, and tools. We reserve this area to the spirits of the forest by leaving it intact, without drawing from its resources. Leaving this space off-limits keeps us mindful of our reliance upon it. In some villages, we perform annual ceremonies for our sacred wood.

We also honor sacred wood at the base of our trees. The spirits of the trees help to bring rain; they communicate when they are thirsty. We offer milk or sacrifice a chicken or goat and pray. We will not level a tree without first making offerings to the spirits that live in it so they will leave the site. Every tree possesses a different level of nyama. Whenever one cuts down a tree, one must appease the nyama through sacrifice; otherwise it can greatly harm the carver, or the entire community. Our shamans and blacksmiths know which trees require what kind of sacrifice. When we cut trees for our ritual objects, the tree must be cut on certain days and at times of the year, and fall in a specific direction.

Some trees possess special meanings in our communities. The sunsun tree (*Diospyros mespiliformis*) is the tree of abundance, and the sana tree (*Daniella oliveri*) is a symbol of long life. The balanza tree (*Acacia albida*) is a symbol of the male component of creation, and connects the heavens and the earth. We do not rest under the shade of this powerful tree without taking precaution. Pregnant women make offerings of shea butter at this tree, which will aid them during their labor.

The kalakari tree (*Heeria insignis*), the tree of luck, is known to respond to one's petitions. When a woman is experiencing difficulty finding a suitable mate, she may wash using the powdered bark of the kalakari. One may also chew the bark of the kalakari and then speak his or her wishes, which may be granted.

One must always clean one's hands with water after touching wood before one eats; otherwise, it can bring sickness to the mouth. The vast amounts of nyama that reside in wood, along with the inhabiting spirits, will inhibit our own powerful centers of nyama, our mouths, if we do not show our appreciation for these givers of the earth.

In every village, we take special care in the construction of our own sacred living spaces. Every land has an owner, a spirit, whom we must befriend if we want to move into its space. We must always make a sacrifice of a goat or a sheep where we wish to build our house. The nyama of the blood of the animal serves as a powerful foundation on which we may construct our dwelling, and brings peace between ourselves and the spirits. Some areas of land require more sacrifice than others, as there may reside a stubborn spirit or spirits who require more appeasing to move from their space. Sometimes a spirit may choose to continue to reside peacefully at the location and provide blessings and protection for the new inhabitants. We know there is a restless spirit among us if we experience an unusual amount of illness or misfortune in the house.

Whatever kind of spirits may occupy our homes, we understand that we are likely to see them if we quietly walk about in the middle of the night. If we awake late in the evening, we always warn the spirits with a knock or loud noise before we enter an unoccupied room. This is a common practice among us to alert spirits of our presence so we do not disturb them.

If a disruptive spirit inhabits our home, we will consult with a diviner to see what sacrifice we must perform in order to appease it or secure its departure. A family member will often dream about a sacrifice if there is an unsatisfied spirit lingering around the house. We may also have a family member among us with a troubled spirit who is keeping the auspicious spirits at bay. A spirit medium will help to determine if this is the source of disturbance in the house.

An effective remedy to ward off spirits who are disrupting a home is to place the fruit of the nponponpogolon tree (*Calotropis procera*) around the outside of the house. We also add millet to the inside of this fruit and bury it in the ground near the home for general prosperity and abundance. Sometimes we tie a bundle of kunjé above the door of our homes, or hang up a worn-down horseshoe to keep away harmful spirits.

The positioning of one's house can greatly affect the inhabitants. We do not build a house along a road at the point where another road ends. We believe that this kind of intersection attracts stagnant spirits. The end of the road is not where one wants to dwell; it is not open to new possibilities and beginnings.

In most of our villages, we save our ceremonies until the dry season. Rain keeps us indoors and is the time for collecting ourselves. We reserve our celebrations for the season of abundance. We dance, we drum, and we connect with our surroundings in gratitude during this time. We celebrate the life that the earth has brought forth. We celebrate the lives of those who have crossed over during the past season. This is a special time when we give thanks for all of our blessings.

Initiation Societies

Initiation societies, or secret societies, are important for the health and well-being of our communities. In our secret societies, we receive some of the highest forms of knowledge. We submit to tests of endurance, courage, and intelligence. We learn to master forces of the visible and invisible worlds. We acquire knowledge of plants, animals, and spirits to improve the condition of human existence on earth. We study the powers of speech and music and are taught how to perform various rituals. In some instances, we have to learn a secret language. In general, we must take an oath of secrecy, and not reveal what we have learned. We pledge to uphold our tradition.

Throughout one's life, starting at the age of seven, one may belong to a secret society. These societies bond the members of each age group to one another for life. Most of our initiation societies are for our men, helping them to attain mystical powers that women naturally possess through their capacities to bring forth and nurture life.

9
Music, Dance
& Ceremony

Self-mastery is the fruit of self-knowledge.

Music and dance are the universal languages of
Spirit, communicating its poetry through celebration, ritual, initiation, and healing. With our instruments and movements, we express our joy and our
sorrow. When we sing, dance, and drum we become
in tune with the harmonious vibrations of the universe. Repetitions of the rhythms become our
mantras.

Many of our community ceremonies begin on
Thursday evening and end on Saturday. As the ceremony progresses, the spirits of music and dance
take over. The drummer beats the drum, and the
spirit of the drum moves the drummer. The dancer
glides through the steps, and the spirit of music
awakens in the dancer. The spirit of song chants

through the singer. Drummer, dancer, and singer are all moved by Spirit.

In our ceremonies, we communicate not only with the spirits, but with one another. Musicians experience the movements of the dancers' bodies and interpret them on the drums; dancers feel the rhythms and interpret them with their movements. We dialogue with one another. Any skilled drummer will be able to dance well and any skilled dancer will be able to play the rhythms of the dance.

Every profession has its own music and dance. Just as we play music for the workers, the workers play music with their work. The hunters dance the actions of their prey. Farmers dance the movements of their sowing and harvests. With their mortar and pestles, women drum out rhythms as they beat and mix their ingredients. We play to increase the satisfaction and productivity in performing every task.

We tell stories through our music and dance that reveal our histories, and the purpose of our lives. Any story is not without music, dance, and ceremony to accompany its performance. The singing and dancing illuminate many parts of the message.

Most importantly, we heal through our music and dance. Dance invites the presence of certain spirits that help those among us who are ill. We dance out our illnesses and pain. We dance and drum for hours to bring about community healing and wholeness. Sometimes we play music to make amends with the spirits for any of our disruptive actions or behaviors. We engage music and dance for everything.

Instruments

We believe the spirits revealed certain instruments to us; they provided us the tools with which to speak to them.

Balafon

A divinity introduced the balafon to Sumanguru Kante, the thirteenth-century Mande king of the Soso tribe of present-day Guinea. Sumanguru saw and heard the balafon in his dreams and awoke to create one. The balafon is a wooden xylophone with gourd resonators. Before we make a new balafon or before we take a balafon out of its storehouse, we make a sacrifice to obtain the spirit's permission to play this sacred instrument. We consult with the spirit mediums in our communities who will let us know what type of sacrifice the spirit wants. We may pour a wine libation or sacrifice a chicken.

We play the balafon at all of our religious ceremonies and often use it at our funerals. Like the flute, it is an instrument that attracts reptiles and snakes to our villages. Harmonious music calms the animals and the spirits; disharmonious music agitates them. We sometimes burn herbs to offset music that our children are learning how to play.

Bafoko and Bolon

We have two instruments that we formerly played when our soldiers went into battle; they are the bafoko and the bolon. The bafoko is an instrument which often accompanies the balafon. We make a bafoko with a large calabash covered loosely by a goatskin. The bolon is a unique instrument with three strings and a gourd resonator, which we play as both a harp and a drum. Many of our musicians play this instrument at naming ceremonies.

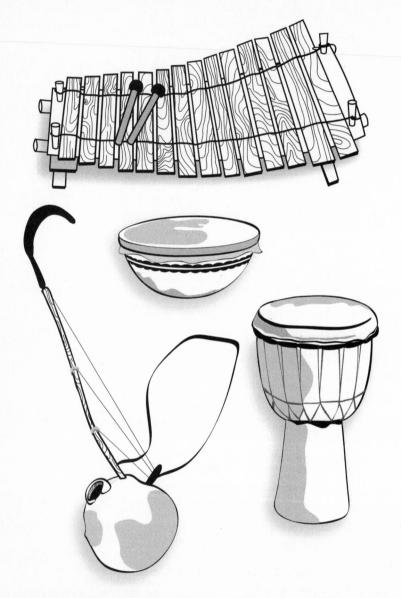

The instruments above are among those used in West African communities. The balafon (top) is a wooden version of the xylophone. The
bafoko (center) is made from a calabash gourd, covered with goatskin.
The three-stringed bolon (lower left) has a gourd resonator, serving as
both a harp and a drum. The jembé (lower right) has a goatskin top,
tightened with lacing in traditional patterns.

Jembé

The jembé is one of the most common drums found throughout West Africa, originating from the Mali and Guinea regions. In Bamana, jembé means to come together and share the music. To play the jembé well, is to speak a Mande language with the rhythms. To appreciate the sounds of the jembé, is to receive the deep message of its communicating rhythms.

We often play the jembé suspended from straps clasped about the shoulders. The skin is strong and contains the soul and energy of a goat, so we must appease the goat's nyama before we play this instrument. The skin on this hour-glass drum can break if we make love right before we perform with it. We do not play this instrument when the sun is hot or setting as roaming spirits are active during these times.

There are three basic strokes we play on the jembé: "slap," "tone," and "bass." We play the jembé as both a solo and an accompanying instrument. We wash our hands with special herbs to prevent their roughness and blistering when we drum. To make our hands strong and pure, in order to produce a clean, spiritual sound, we gather seven branches from various bushes and boil them in water to soak and wash our hands in. The branches must come from more than one bush, and they must be touching the ground when they are picked. We choose the branches that like to sweep the earth when the winds from the heavens blow. These branches have a special affinity with the heavens and the earth and washing with them spiritually grounds us.

Jun-juns

Jun-juns are a set of three, two-headed drums made of wood and cowhides that often accompany jembé playing. The jun-juns provide the bass of the music. The kinkini is the smallest of the three jun-juns, the sangwa is the medium-sized drum, and the jun-jun is the largest of them all. Usually we play our jun-juns with sticks. In some communities, only bards may play these drums. Elsewhere, jun-juns do not have hereditary restrictions on who may play them.

Kora, Ngoni, and Balafon

The kora, the ngoni, and the balafon are the three fundamental melody instruments of the bard. Depending on the region, one of the three instruments will take precedence. In Gambia, the

This kora, made for children, is referred to as a baby kora.

kora rules; in Mali, it is the ngoni, and in Guinea, the balafon. The kora looks and sounds something like a harp. It is made of a calabash gourd cut in half and partially covered with cowskin and has twenty-one playing strings. We may use fishing line for the strings. The ngoni is the Mande name for an ancient traditional lute found throughout West Africa that usually has either four or seven strings.

Sabar

Sabar is both a style of dance and an orchestra of hand and stick drums of the Wolof people of Senegal. The skin drums are played with one hand and a thin wooden stick. One may play it while it is set on the ground or strapped to the side of the body. Sabar speaks the languages of the Wolof and Serer peoples. There are many styles of sabar dancing. We now play jembé variations for some of the sabar rhythms.

Rhythms

We have hundreds of rhythms that musicians throughout West Africa know, and each of these rhythms tells its own story. A drummer must be knowledgeable of the meanings of the rhythms to speak effectively with the drum. Each jembé rhythm and dance has a purpose, a time, and a place. Some of our rhythms honor groups of people, other rhythms mark certain occasions. Some people are susceptible to particular rhythms that invite a spirit upon them.

Dala

Dala is a Guinean rhythm we play to honor our women fishers. We play dala to protect the fisherwomen from any harmful spirits in the open waters.

Denbadon

Denbadon consists of several rhythms and dances we play during popular festivities to show reverence to our mothers. Den means "child," ba means "mother," and "don" is dance.

Dundunba

This is a Guinean rhythm that honors the strong and the brave among us. There are more than fifty dundunba rhythms. We name the rhythm after the jun-juns (or dun-duns) because these drums provide the lead rhythm while the jembé accompanies them. Sometimes our dancers perform great acrobats and show potential spouses and the elders of the village their vitality and bravery. Women dance specific movements for these rhythms. In the past we played dundunba to settle disputes among the men of the villages.

Jansa

Also known as *bara*, jansa is a popular rhythm originating from Mali. We perform it in the evening for many celebrations, and especially for the full moon, spring equinox, and summer and winter solstices. We also play jansa at our harvest and wedding celebrations. We begin the rhythm slowly, picking up speed when a talented dancer moves into the middle of the circle. Great dancers sometimes manipulate a pestle while dancing jansa.

Kakilambé

Kakilambé is a Guinean rhythm that honors the spirit kakilambé. The spirit of the kakilambé is a protector against disruptive spirits, and appears to the community to relay important messages. As the drummers speed up the rhythm, the spirit medium receives the information. Afterward, the diviner relays the message of the kakilambé. Only the initiated dancer may see the kakilambé who will visit from the bush to communicate helpful messages for the safety and prosperity of the village. We also play this rhythm as a welcoming song and dance.

Kassa

Also known as *susu*, kassa is a traditional harvest dance and rhythm of the Malinké people. We play this rhythm for those working in the fields to accompany their cultivation and harvest of the crops. The workers often must walk for miles and we play kassa as they walk from field to field. In Gambia, we play it to accompany workers as they tap palm trees for sap to make palm wine. We drum and dance kassa to celebrate a bountiful harvest at a festival called the kassaladon.

Komo

Komo is a drum rhythm and a sacred mask dance of the blacksmiths who carved the early jembé drums. *Komadon* is the dance that accompanies this rhythm; it is the dance of the secret society komo. We play this song for those who experience spirit possessions or mental challenges.

Koreduga

This is a Malian rhythm we play for the Koreduga, a Bamana people whose role in our celebrations and festivities is to make the crowd laugh using mimicry, impersonations, and acrobatics. This rhythm accompanies the dances of our community clowns.

Kuku

Kuku comes from Guinea and was traditionally a rhythm we played for our boy initiates when they returned to the community after their circumcision rites of passage. Parents would dance kuku to welcome home their sons from their initiations. We play this rhythm for the end of the harvest festivities and for all other joyous occasions. Today there are many ways to drum kuku.

Lamba

The lamba is the bard dance and is a rhythm we play at major rites of passage ceremonies, such as births, circumcisions, marriages, and funerals. When the village elders come before us on important occasions at planting or harvest times, we dance the lamba, in honor of our ancestors and Spirit.

Liberté

Also known as ligueba, liberté is a rhythm from Guinea. This new rhythm became popular after Guinea gained its independence from French rule in 1958. Liberté is popular at festivals and is a competition rhythm for ballet schools.

Manjani

Manjani is a rhythm coming from the border of Mali and Guinea. We play manjani on festive occasions. It is an initiation and celebration dance that we perform at rites of passage ceremonies for our children passing into adulthood. We play manjani to test the skills of the dancers. A manjani is what we sometimes call the best young female dancer of a village.

Maraka or Marakadon

Maraka is a baptism and marriage rhythm originating from Mali. Marakadon is performed mostly by women during popular celebrations. We use only one jembé and a single kinkini to play this rhythm.

Moribiassa

The Moribiassa is a rhythm we play on very specific occasions. Mostly, we play this rhythm for the return of a special person whom we have not seen in many years, whether they are a living individual or an ancestor. Women dance moribiassa at the crossroads to petition the spirit for the healing of a loved one who is ill or experiencing mental challenges. We also make promises that we will dance moribiassa if the spirits grant us something we ask of them.

Ngrin

Ngrin is the mother of all the rhythms originating from Mali. We play this complex rhythm for festive occasions such as naming and marriage ceremonies. Ngrin is also known as the rhythm of shamans.

Soko

Soko originates from Guinea. We perform this rhythm in the evening for our young boys before they leave for their circumcision initiation. We shave the heads of these children who will be circumcised, and the drummers play soko afterward.

Soli

Soli comes from Guinea and is a rhythm for the circumcision of boys and girls. Many different regions have their own version of soli and we do not always play it for circumcisions. In the public gathering areas, the singing and drumming invites people to perform the popular dance that accompanies this rhythm.

Sorsoner

The sorsoner rhythm comes from the Baga people of Guinea. Young girls dance this rhythm in the full moonlight to show respect for their mothers.

Sunu

This is an old rhythm that originates from Mali. In the village of Sagabari, there was a beautiful young woman named Sunu Mamady. Everyone loved her and appreciated her wonderful dancing. No festivity could take place without her participation. This rhythm was created in her honor by a jembé players' troupe from her village. When we play this rhythm, it is an opportunity for young girls to demonstrate their grace, beauty, and strength. We also play sunu at marriages and other festivals.

Yankadi

Yankadi is a dance and courting rhythm of the people of Guinea. The word "yankadi" translates to yan (here) + ka di (is sweet). Yankadi is a rhythm we play for a social dance, which we call a yankadi. In the dance four couples at a time dance with one another and briefly with other partners.

10
FAMILY

*All that one has one owes once to one's
father, and twice to one's mother.*

We identify one another by our family names.[1] Our
families are watched over by our ancestors and led
by our elders. Everyone within the family unit has
his or her own special role and contribution to
make. We observe this understanding of the family and believe that veering from it is disruptive to
the unity and harmony of the community.

In the village, each child is everyone's child, and
each family member a part of everyone's family. If
someone from the village marries one from another
village, both villages become family. This is not just
what we say or believe, this is how we live. If someone from another village needs help with some kind
of work, all of the men from both villages will join
together to accomplish it. If a child from one village
needs guidance or help, members of the nearby villages will be available to provide it.

As we respect the elders in our communities, so we respect the eldest among us within our families. We defer to those who are older; they are those who look after us and who hold more responsibility. What belongs to them belongs to us. We may borrow anything from an older relative without asking. They may request that we perform certain tasks, which we will perform joyfully. We strive to lovingly be of assistance to the eldest among us.

What our older relatives teach us is precious. The small ways that we may help them cannot compare to the teachings and support they provide to us. We do not think of ourselves as performing a duty or obligation. We defer to those older than us to let them know that we appreciate their guidance and all they have to offer.

Older relatives will always forsake their own needs for ours. We show respect to our older brother, knowing that he will be the first to shield us in times of danger. We honor our oldest sister, knowing that she will be the one to feed us before herself in times of hunger. The oldest among us are the first to leave the table and save the last bit of food for those who are younger.

Family relations are broad in our communities. A child will have more than one set of parents, and know many women as "mother," and many men as "father." If our mother has any sisters, they are our mothers too. By extension, our mother's sisters' children are our brothers and sisters. Our father's brothers are our fathers also. A man's wives include those of his brothers' and a woman's husbands include those of her sisters. Should a man's brother pass away, he may marry his brother's wife. This is true for a woman and her sister's husband as well. We practice this observance so that we always keep our families intact and together. Grandparents, aunts, uncles, cousins, and siblings all share in the instruction, support, and nurturing of a child. No child will grow without love and guidance.

When our children grow up, they return the care to those who nurtured them to adulthood. Children maintain a humility about their limited time in this world, and naturally defer to their elders who have suffered, endured, and helped to bring them into this life. When a woman marries, she moves from the home of her parents to live with her husband's family, which is now her own. She will care for her husband's mother, as her own mother cared for her. She will cook for her, clean for her, and relieve her of the duties of caring for the family. Now it is her mother's opportunity to relax, enjoy her grandchildren, and all the fruits of her labor. A son will remain with his mother for the remainder of her life, providing financial stability and support. As the husband often passes before a wife, the son will now take the responsibility of his father, caring for and looking after his mother.

Men and women maintain their own special roles in our communities.[2] Women care for the children, cook, garden, and sometimes help in tending to the livestock. Many times, they will sell their produce and arts and crafts in the marketplace and contribute to the family fund. Men provide financial support, maintain the structure of the house, hunt, and handle relations with other families. Women hold the powers and secrets for bringing forth life; both men and women possess their own special knowledge for maintaining it. We respect the roles that men and women hold in our communities and show special reverence to our mothers for all of their love, work, and support.

We come into this life with eternal appreciation for our being. We cannot repay our parents for our existence, though we will spend our lives trying. We do not compare our families to others. We do not look at what we did or did not receive as children. We learn not to hold grudges within our families or harbor anger. We grow up experiencing that all the responsibility for nurturing and support does not rest solely with our parents. What our father cannot offer us, our uncle will. What our sister may not give us, our cousin can. Everyone in the family makes a significant contribution to our growth and development, and for this we are ever grateful. Nothing can divide the strong bonds of the family.

Breaking Bread

Eating together is a special ritual experience that serves to bring peace and unity among us in our families and in our communities. When we eat, usually the men eat from one bowl and the women and children eat from another. There may be up to twenty of us, and we eat from the same dish, experiencing the joy of feasting together. We eat sitting on the floor to be close to the earth. Our crumbs fall to the ground as offerings for our ancestors. We eat with our hands to better taste the food and to feel a direct connection with the fruits of the earth. The youngest among us may rest a finger or thumb on the bowl as we all eat to show respect to the elders.

We wash our hands from one bowl of water, often in a calabash that we pass around the circle before and after we eat. After the meal, we may sprinkle the water in front of our doorway for blessings. We always welcome guests to join us in our feasting and never turn anyone away who is hungry. It is forbidden in our communities to turn anyone away for a meal, or to complain about the cost or amount of food. It is a blessing for us to have the opportunity to share our abundance with each other.

When a woman carries a pot of food, she must touch it to the ground when she passes a man. If she is carrying an empty pot she will always carry it with one hand. If one borrows a pot from somebody, one will first place it on the ground before returning it to the owner. These acts imbue the food and cookware with blessings, and pay homage to the earth for its bounty.

11
PREGNANCY
& BIRTH

A human being is the universe in miniature.

Fertility

In the village, our survival depends upon the fertility of our land and the proliferation of our families. Abundant crops, robust livestock, and plentiful vegetation keep our communities healthy and strong. We value the fertility of all living beings and engage many rituals to ensure the fecundity of the earth and her creatures. Women's fertility is especially celebrated, as it is our children who will secure the future of our families. Our children care for us when we grow old and they help to ensure our transition into the realm of the ancestors.

An infertile individual is one who sometimes suffers a great burden in our communities. Infertility can result from many things, such as disharmony in the home between a woman and her husband.

When a woman has difficulty conceiving, she may perform different rituals or offer special prayers to improve her opportunities for having a child. Fish, tortoises, snakes, panthers, and leopards are animals that represent feminine power, and an infertile woman may make use of them in a fertility ritual. She may make her offerings at the base of the baobab tree for fertility. A woman usually makes offerings to Muso Koroni, the mother of creation, chaos, and mystical practices.[1] Muso Koroni has many breasts and sometimes appears as a black panther or leopard, causing women to menstruate by scratching them with her claws.

A mask of Muso Koroni, the beloved mother of creation and chaos.

A woman who cannot conceive may consume various herbs, including the bark and fruit of ntoro with a porridge made from millet. She will eat it four straight days for infertility. An infertile woman may also crush the unripe fruit of ntoro and mix it with mandesunsun into a powder to consume daily. A man may also consume mandesunsun along with other herbs for impotence, or he will eat a meat soup containing the powdered bark of ntomi.

Often a couple who cannot conceive will consult a diviner to determine the cause. Sometimes they will not have children if someone else has enacted powerful charms to hinder their fertility. Sometimes a particular spirit may be possessive of either the woman or man. Many women who receive the calling of healing or divination in our communities are often unable to produce children. These special women have another kind of role in our communities with a great opportunity to mother and nurture us with their mystical gifts and insights.

Pregnancy Observances

The ways of a woman during her pregnancy determine the ways of her unborn child. A pregnant woman will observe many practices to protect herself and her baby. She will not walk outside when the sun is setting, nor when the sun is hot overhead, or late at night, as roaming spirits are active during these times. A pregnant woman will no longer work in the fields, nor visit the bush where powerful nature spirits abound. A woman will not lay down with her belly facing the light of the moon, which emits too much nyama. She does not let others touch her stomach as people possess different kinds of energy that may not be wholesome for the baby.

Many women consume herbs every day for a healthy, peaceful pregnancy. One popular practice is to boil the roots of ntoro with other plants and drink the concoction during pregnancy. Most often, pregnant women consume kolobé for well-being throughout their pregnancy. Drinking kolobé, without sugar, three times a day can help with pregnancy diabetes.

Most women wear amulets and talismans during their pregnancy to keep away harmful nyama and forces, and to invite peaceful energy and spirits their way. A pregnant woman must not see blood or monstrous types of things that may be disturbing to the unborn child. One who often looks down at her belly will have a child who looks like her. When a woman is pregnant, she will often refrain from intimacy with her husband. Pregnancy is a sacred time for the baby to receive the mother's nurturing and attention.

The father has his own special bond with his child, as the child receives both parents' nyama. A father may loosen his belt during the mother's pregnancy to help establish his connection with the child, mother, and the pregnancy. A father's tight belt may inhibit the growth of the child. Sometimes, during the mother's labor, the father will have his belt loosely wrapped around the mother's waist as an offering of his own nyama and support for the child's entry into the world. The pains that a mother feels during labor, the father may feel as well through the connection of the belt.

The father is not to kill nor assist in the killing of any animal until after the birth of the child. A carpenter will not drive a nail, which could cause a difficult labor for his wife. He may perform all other tasks belonging to his craft, but he must have an assistant to drive the nails. A soon-to-be father must not take a hoe and clear a cemetery path, which exposes him to harmful levels of nyama.

During pregnancy neither parent should eat the flesh of any animal that was itself pregnant upon its death, nor should they eat an animal's intestines, bowels, liver, or heart. The potent concentration of nyama within these body parts can create difficulties for the developing baby. Parents never name the child nor think of names for the unborn baby until after its birth. Naming a child before it is born shows presumption; it does not show proper reverence to the unknown and mysterious power of the spirit world, which may decide to keep the baby for itself. A family can ask a diviner if the unborn child is a boy or a girl, but most parents wait until the child is born.

A woman whose child remains in the womb longer than nine months is often thought to be an extraordinary being. This superhealer or shaman comes into the world rich with great potential. Extraordinary circumstances such as an extended pregnancy manifests higher levels of nyama, which the child carries into this world.[2]

Time of Birth

No man may enter the room where a woman is giving birth. Giving birth is a sacred act of which women are the guardians and keepers. Bringing a life into the world is a woman's special power, and such knowledge is not the affairs of a man. A woman in labor receives support from her sisters, aunts, mothers, and grandmothers during this time. The women will encourage her, nurture her, and massage her body with shea butter to help relax her. They may also bring her to the balanza tree (*Acacia albida*) and make offerings of shea oil as a petition for its assistance in easing her labor.

The midwife works with great amounts of nyama when the child is born, so she equips herself with powerful herbs, incantations, amulets, and talismans. The midwife immediately cleans the child off before uniting the baby with the mother. The afterbirth contains so much nyama that the midwife must remove it before the mother and child are brought together.

The baby's first bath is important and serves to remove the great amounts of energy a newborn possesses. The mother, or an elder, will remove nyama from the baby by gently blowing into the ears and quickly sucking at the nose or mouth and navel, spitting afterward on the ground to release it. A woman in the family will continue to perform this ritual bath daily to release a baby's nyama for the first few months of the child's life.

Caring for Mother

The mother also receives a bath from her sisters and women elders; they massage her body with shea butter, and dip a cloth in warm water containing the balanza bark, to rub her body down for healing. Family and friends will sing a song to her that she may continue to hear for the months ahead:

> *Thank you to our children's mothers*
> *Thank you to our children's mothers*
> *Thank you to all of our mothers*
> *Thank you to all of our mothers*
> *They are those who are blessed*
> *They are those who care for us*
> *It is not easy*
> *It is not easy to give life*

Newborn Care

A woman will not leave the house for a week after the birth of her baby. This first week of a newborn's life is a special time for the mother and baby to bond. The infant is vulnerable to energy and spirits in the world, and the mother uses this delicate time to drink special herbs and medicines with her baby. The mother may feed her baby medicines with animal bones to give the child the strength and power of these creatures of the bush. One protective herb for our children is the jala plant (*Khaya senegalensis*). We cut a twig from this plant and tie it around the waists of our newborns for the first week of their lives, to protect them from harmful forces and spirits. We may feed our children the jala plant when they are ill. Adults, too, sometimes drink water with jala bark to cure a stomachache.

Once the umbilical cord is cut, the parents may ritually bury it along with the placenta at the east gate of the village. Women may also bury or hang their placenta around the balanza tree as a gesture of appreciation for its assistance during their labor. Both the umbilical cord and placenta are powerful fertility talismans and have many uses in our gardens and fields to nourish abundance.

We mix clay with shea butter and place it on the child's belly to help the cord fall off in the first week. We may keep this cord as medicine for the child. Whenever the child has a stomachache, we dip the cord in water (three times for boys; four times for girls) for the child to drink for a remedy.

Twins

As the birth of twins is an extraordinary occurrence in our communities, we treat them as unique and mysterious spirits who carry special messages from the spirit world. Twins are the children of the spirit of water, Faro—the spirit who reflects, like a mirror, the shadow or double of creation. We often perform the naming ceremonies for our twins at the river, where we wash them. When we shave their heads, we throw their hair back into the waters. The day of the twins' naming ceremony, the father will also offer a special prayer to the twins on bended knees, requesting their special protection to the family. Divination may also accompany the twins' birth to determine what exceptional gifts they bring to their family. We often reserve special names for our twins.[3] We call the parents of twins "lucky ones."

We construct a small protective altar for our twins, over which the father presides and makes sacrifice. Sometimes parents of twins pass down their twins' altars to the parents of a new set of twins. The twins' altar consists of two cones, with a piece of the twins' umbilical cord bound around the center. We hang the altar above the outside entrance of our homes. We place the altar on high, as with our other family altars, so that it will not make contact with the earth, water, or fire, which reduces its nyama.

We make yearly sacrifices on this altar, as well as sacrifices before and after the rainy season, and during all of the major rites of passage of the twins' lives. We offer or sacrifice two of everything, one for each twin. We offer two white kola nuts, two balls of millet, and millet beer. We will also sacrifice two white chickens, pouring their blood and the alcoholic libations over the umbilical cord of the altar. We pour our offerings twice, one for each child.

The scorpion is the twin's protective creature, and some of us believe that the existence of the twin's altar allows any twin, or their mother, to handle a scorpion without being stung. Scorpions may also sting those who attempt to harm the twins. The second twin born is truly the oldest sibling who sends the younger one into the world to give his or her initial impressions of it.

If one of a pair of twins dies at a young age, the parents may construct a wooden image of the twin and place it alongside the living child during sleep. The image helps to comfort the remaining child and also contains special medicines and power to ward off any lingering danger. Any time the child receives any gifts, offerings of cowrie shells will be made to the twin statue.

Death of a Child

The death of a child is a powerful message from the spirit world that we heed seriously. We observe the actions of the parents, family members, and friends to understand who may harbor harmful attitudes or behaviors. We look at our sacrifices and offerings to see if we need to make more. We explore ourselves and our relationship to the environment to see if we have offended spirits or one another.

A family who has lost an infant may give a future child a name that the spirits will not like, such as "ragged clothes," "garbage," or "the person no one likes." These names tell the spirits that the family is not attached to the child. When we show the spirits we want our children too much, they may want them for themselves. To really want something is to attract spirits and tempt them into giving us lessons of gratitude, humility, and detachment.

After the death of a child, a family may also pierce a baby's ear or make a small cut near the sides of the eyes to mark the child. If this child also dies we look for the signs of a pierced ear or marked face in the next baby to see if it is the spirit of a departed brother or sister. In the burial of a first-born infant, we may make special arrangements, or bury the child with potent charms or items to keep open the possibility of the mother bearing more children.

Child Rearing

A child maintains a close dependence on the mother for thirty-three months. The first nine months take place in the womb and the next twenty-four months are on the mother's breast. Thirty-three is a significant number that equals the number of vertebrae in the spinal column. After this period of nourishment from the mother, a child is ready to stand erect and independent.

Sometimes a family member or close friend of the mother will breast-feed her child. Children who share the same breast milk, even if only once, share the same blood. We view them as siblings who must abide by the same rules and never marry. Those among us nurtured from the same breast will sometimes refer to each other as "breast milk," acknowledging the deep bond that results from sharing this sacred, life-giving substance.

Massage is an important ritual in caring for a child. We massage our children and stretch their limbs daily to release harmful nyama and keep them flexible. We begin the massage by melting shea butter and rubbing it all over the baby's body. We massage the neck and the back, then the torso and limbs. We pick up the child by both arms and then hold the baby by each arm. We pick up the baby by both legs, and then by each leg. We stretch the child's feet up to the ears, and massage the body until it is quite flexible. We then gently toss the baby in the air three times with a gentle sway. We massage our children every morning for at least the first six months of their lives.

We draw black eyebrows on our newborns, using a paste of burnt dates. Dark eyebrows ward off harmful spirits, protect the eyes from sickness and absorb anything negative the child might see. A parent may observe this practice for the first few months of an infant's life. Once the baby begins teething, the child may wear fish teeth around the neck to ease the pain. When our children lose their first teeth, we toss their teeth up on our rooftops with a prayer for blessings. We throw our children's teeth high into the sky to signify growth and longevity. The birds pick up the teeth and carry them away to aid the new growth and transition. We sometimes tie the toenail of a pig around the legs of our children to help them walk earlier. We place a knife, wrapped in a blanket, under our baby's sleeping head for protection.

When a child coughs, we always say the word "tokho" two or three times. The word does not have any specific meaning; it is simply a special sound that penetrates the chest of the baby to make it strong. The power of the adult's chest sends energy to that of the child's with the word "tokho."

A mother always carries her baby on her back, not on her chest. This allows her to continue her work without disturbance to the child or her work. Mothers carry their babies on their backs also to show the children how to follow and respect them. We tell our children the story of Baylo to teach them the importance of respecting their parents.

The Story & Song of Baylo

A beautiful woman, Sirajan, was known throughout the land for her generosity, kindness, and open heart. The day Sirajan was ready to leave home and marry, the women elders of the village gave her a gold calabash. This sacred gift was unlike any gift given to a woman for her marriage; because Sirajan was an extraordinary woman in the community, always helping others, she was offered this unique present.

Eventually Sirajan had her own children, and Baylo was her first daughter. Baylo did not learn the lessons of generosity and kindness that her mother tried to teach her by example. The day Baylo was to marry, she asked her mother for her gold calabash. Sirajan always gave generously to her children, but this time she did not let Baylo have her way. She sang:

> *Baylo, you cannot have my gold calabash,*
> *Baylo, me, I have this calabash from my generosity,*
>   *kindness, and open heart,*
> *Baylo, you cannot have my gold calabash,*
> *Baylo, me, I have this calabash from my generosity,*
>   *kindness, and open heart,*

Baylo, I went to see the male village elders, and they told me
one word,[4]
Baylo, me, I have this calabash from my generosity,
kindness, and open heart,
Baylo, I went to see the female village elders, and they
showed me their pendelou,[5]
Baylo, me, I have this calabash from my generosity,
kindness, and open heart,
Baylo, I went to see the village children, and they came with
their slingshots,[6]
Baylo, me, I have this calabash from my generosity,
kindness, and open heart,
Baylo you cannot have my gold calabash,
Baylo, me, I have this calabash from my generosity,
kindness, and open heart,
Baylo, me, I have this calabash from my generosity,
kindness, and open heart,
Baylo, me, I have this calabash from my generosity,
kindness, and open heart.

Naming Ceremony

African names carry special meaning, and when we name a child it is a profound experience. The chosen name may be one of an ancestor whom the child resembles, or one that reflects the family's legacy, or their honored leaders or prophets. One week after the birth of a child, we celebrate the naming with a special ceremony. The name defines the new life and locates the child within the larger community. The naming ceremony is the time when our children experience their spiritual births.

The day of the ceremony, we make offerings of kola nuts and porridge to our family and friends. We serve roselle and kolobé drinks. Both the parents' bards are present at the celebration and sing the praises of each family.

During the ceremony, a family member shaves the head of the newborn. Most of us shave the entire head, others of us leave a little hair on top. We shave the hair as a symbol of rebirth for the child, who is now no longer in the womb but a part of the community and world at large. New growth and fresh beginnings are the intent behind this practice. Sometimes we mix the hair with porridge and bury it in the ground, creating a unity between the child and the earth. Next we split open the kola nuts and give the baby a name. Some of us pour water or alcohol onto the earth or in a calabash three times for a libation. After we announce the name, we make the sacrifice of an animal such as a white goat or sheep.

In some traditions, we place the baby in a plate basket with a blanket and show the baby around to those at the ceremony. The women may rhythmically pound the pestle inside the mortar as the baby is danced around the gathering. Sometimes, we play certain rhythms for certain names.

Identity in our communities is significant. Our name is our history and our bloodline. If we do not have anyone who knows us, we are lost spirits. Our naming ceremonies give us the opportunity to receive our identities and make them known to the entire community. We tell the story of Sanfin Diallo to teach our children the value of identity and the importance of the naming ceremony.

The Story of Sanfin Diallo

A long time ago, in a village far away, a child was born. One week later, following the custom in our land, the young boy was given a naming ceremony. During the ceremony, the family members passed the baby around in a basket for all to see. As the mother held the basket, the bards announced the baby's new name, "Sanfin Diallo." The moment the bards called out "Sanfin Diallo," the spirits lifted the baby in his basket high up to the heavens. Sanfin Diallo completely disappeared out of sight and none of his family ever saw him again.

Forty-five years later, when the spirits let Sanfin return to his village, they sent him back with money, gold, and jewelry. Sanfin bought a big house in the village, and many animals for his home. Almost no one who attended his naming ceremony was still living. Not one person remembered Sanfin Diallo . . . except for one old lady named Musokura, who was at his naming that day forty-five years ago. Only Musokura saw the naming of Sanfin Diallo, and this old lady lived away from the village. She slept outside and kept to herself.

One day, Sanfin Diallo decided he wanted to marry. He told all the bards that he would like a wife, but he would only marry the woman who knew his true identity. The bards made the announcement to the entire village that Sanfin Diallo wanted to marry somebody, but that the woman must know his name. Even the bards themselves did not know Sanfin Diallo's name.

There was great excitement over the ceremony. Many women hoped for the opportunity to marry this prince. For days, women prepared for the ceremony, fixing their hair, sewing their clothes, and making themselves as beautiful as they could. Even though no one knew the identity of Sanfin Diallo, they were all going to try to guess his name.

Next door to this village lived a humble family with very little money. In this family, a young, single woman named Nyeleni heard about the big event in the neighboring village. Nyeleni wanted to attend the ceremony but she did not have any special clothes to wear. Her mother encouraged her to go to the festivities anyway. With old, torn clothes, Nyelini made her way to the village to attend the ceremony for the prince. Since she was coming from another village, she was the last one in line.

In the meantime, Musokura, who knew of the identity of Sanfin Diallo, sat along the side of the road, as all the ladies walked by her to attend the ceremony. Many passed right by the old woman, who had dirtied and bruised herself after taking a hard fall. She asked every young woman who passed her by to help her. Each woman continued on her way, thinking of herself and whether she would successfully become the bride of Sanfin Diallo.

Eventually, Nyelini passed Musokura on the street, and immediately stopped to help her. Forgetting her own needs to get to the ceremony quickly, Nyelini went back to her home to fetch some food, clean water, and herbs, and bring them to Musokura. When Nyelini returned with the food and medicine, she asked Musokura to pray for her so she could marry the prince. To Nyelini's surprise, Musokura leaned closely to her and in a soft voice said, "The day of the prince's naming ceremony I was there. I know his name and I will give it to you." In her ear, Musokura whispered the name of Sanfin Diallo.

Nyelini thanked Musokura and quickly made her way to the ceremony. Nyelini had a difficult time making her way through the crowd, as all the women pushed her away and did not want to be close to her. They had tried to guess the name of Sanfin Diallo but failed. Only one young woman remained who stood up to guess the name of Sanfin Diallo. Sanfin picked up his ngoni and began to play. The woman sang:

> Your name is Mamadou.
> The long, powerful snake is Mamadou.
> The one we cannot compare with anybody is Mamadou.

Sanfin Diallo, stopped playing his lute, and sadly replied to the woman, "No, my name is not Mamadou." As Sanfin saw this was the last woman in line, he was disheartened. Picking up his lute to return home, Sanfin suddenly heard a shout from the crowd. Nyelini quickly edged her way to the front of the line, and declared, "I would like to try."

Sanfin picked up his lute, once again, and began to play.

In the sweetest voice, the young woman sang:

> Your name is Sanfin Diallo
> The long, powerful snake is Sanfin Diallo
> The one no one can compare to Sanfin Diallo.

Before Nyelini could even finish all of the words to the song, Sanfin Diallo threw his instrument in the air and ran into her arms. Soon after, Sanfin Diallo and Nyelini were married and moved into a home together. Sanfin Diallo and his wife took care of one another and Nyelini's family. They also brought Musokura into their home to live with them happily ever after.

Lessons of Sanfin Diallo

If Sanfin Diallo did not experience the sacred tradition of his naming, he would not have been known to the community. He would have lost his identity completely. The naming ceremony ensures us a place in the world.

The story of Sanfin Diallo also teaches us that the person with the kind and loving heart is always the one who prevails. We must always care for our elders, as they are the keepers of our traditions. We must never deny anybody because of their appearance or what they do not have. This story also demonstrates that in our culture, it is not the husband and wife who live happily ever after, but it is the family who lives happily ever after.

12
CHILDHOOD
INITIATION

To know animals is good.
To know trees is good.
To know oneself is better
than them all.

Our children experience their initiation into adulthood just before or after puberty when they are taught about their social and spiritual responsibilities as men and women. Initiations into manhood or womanhood usually include circumcision. The age for a person to experience childhood initiation has become younger over time. Formerly, our children were ready for initiation in their late teens, but now we may initiate them when they are between eight and twelve years old. With the influence of city life, school, and work abroad, our children are enduring the realities of adulthood at a younger age.[1] Fewer health complications arise, too, the younger our children are when they experience circumcision.

There are many variations for the types of initiations our children experience, especially for the girls. Young women may receive instruction in small groups from their mothers, or they may receive more formal initiations, with a period of ritual seclusion. The childhood rite of passage usually requires the initiate to withdraw from the community for a period of time. The transition from childhood to adulthood is a serious and profound experience, and the departure from the community is challenging and significant. The initiates leave the community as children; they return as adults with all of the virtue and responsibility their new role carries.

Circumcision

Circumcision is a long-standing tradition for our children. In some communities, the circumcision of a child is an induction into a secret society. We always circumcise our boys, and we often circumcise our girls, though this tradition is now waning.[2] For the young girls, there are many different ways to perform the circumcision. In many communities, we excise a small piece the size of a grain as the cut is often only symbolic. Sometimes, now, the children undergo the circumcision in the hospital to minimize any health risks, and experience the initiation afterwards.

The cutting of flesh to release the nyama of childhood and make way for the life of adulthood is an essential component of the initiation. The spilling of blood as a sacrifice to the realm of Spirit for the welcoming of new life is necessary for the transition into adulthood to occur.[3] For young girls, menstruation signals their transition into womanhood, and this may be one reason why the act of circumcision for young girls is carrying less weight than it does for young boys. The young woman naturally spills her blood, whereas a young boy must initiate that cut and spill his blood onto the earth for his transition into adulthood. If he does not, he will never be able to marry or have children. A young boy must experience circumcision if he is ever to come into manhood in traditional Mande society.

Ceremony Preparations

Some villages perform circumcisions for all of the initiates once a year, others perform them every three years. Some of us set the date of the initiation according to the position of Sirius in the sky.[4] For many of us, Venus is the circumcision star, and we will conduct our childhood initiations when this star is at its brightest. The initiations in most villages take place during the dry season.

The celebration before the boys go to the bush or the girls to a secluded home can last up to three months. In some villages, former initiates dance and play certain rhythms the night before the initiation to signal to the community another one is about to occur. In other villages, the boys sleep with their paternal uncles the night before, and awake before the sun rises to enter the bush. We may make a sacrifice of a chicken or an offering of some porridge, which the children will eat the morning of their departure. Sometimes the boys may shave their heads. The oldest usually leads the way to the initiation retreat, and the younger ones follow.

The Rite of Passage

During their months of seclusion, the initiates live away from the community with shamans, diviners, and traditionalists who teach them about the responsibilities and blessings of adulthood. The long excursion away from home prepares the initiates for their rebirth into the community. The initiates learn about cooperation and community building as they live among their peers during this crucial rite of passage. A boy may learn how to care for a family, hunt, and fend for himself. A girl will learn how to care for a family, garden, and manage livestock. The children learn traditional songs and stories. Many things the initiates absorb during this powerful time are secret. The shamans perform sacrifice, and protect the initiates with magical herbs. During the process, each initiate may be given a new name and a new identity.

Every day, the women of the village bring food to the edge of the bush, accompanied by a bard who sounds the drums, signaling the food is ready. The elders in the bush retrieve the food, as newly circumcised boys must not see any women. The boys are given special sticks with a calabash at one end, which is shaken to make a rattling sound. Every day the initiate will make a cut in the stick to know how long he has been in the bush and how long his wound will take to heal.

The initiation helps the young adults to overcome challenges and face their fears. An important ritual for the initiates can include learning how to subdue fire. Special music may accompany this ritual. During this rite of passage, initiates learn to realize their bravery, courage, and strength.

The Story and Song of Modi Bouramani

Modi Bouramani is an historical figure who protects initiates undergoing circumcision by keeping away harmful spirits. Male initiates sing to Modi Bouramani during their time in the forest to give them courage.

> *Modi Bouramani, Modi Bouramani,*
> *When Modi Bouramani died the day did not come,*
> *The day Modi Bouramani died the sun did not rise,*
> *Between the night and the day, the bana tree grew at*
>   *Modi Bouramani's grave,*
> *Between the night and the day, the seben tree grew at*
>   *Modi Bouramani's grave,*
> *If you see the seben tree at his grave, it looks just like*
>   *Modi Bouramani,*
> *If you see the bana tree at his grave, it looks just like*
>   *Modi Bouramani,*
> *Bana, seben, Modi Bouramani, bana, seben,*
>   *Modi Bouramani.*

For the initiates, the seben (*Borassus aethiopum*) and bana trees are symbols of Modi Bouramani. These powerful trees possess many healing purposes in our communities. Every time an initiate passes these trees, he will remember Modi Bouramani and his protective presence; these tall, sturdy trees are also masculine symbols and represent how our young men's bodies will heal and regenerate. Between the night and the day represents the transition between childhood and adulthood. The grave is the place of burial for the initiate's childhood, as he now assumes his new role in the community as a man.

Sacred Act

During the circumcision, the initiate may face the east. For a boy, the circumcision may take place on a mortar or piece of wood. In many villages, the blacksmith circumcises. If not a blacksmith, the one who circumcises is a person with special abilities, medicine, and power to handle the great amounts of nyama given off during the cutting. The circumcisor swiftly cuts the skin with a knife.

For a girl, a woman of the blacksmith group, who is a pottery maker, may conduct the ceremony. She will perform the circumcision in a place where the women make pottery, a place full of nyama. The initiate may sit on an upside-down pot, mortar, or jar, while adult relatives stand behind her for support. The cut is always swift.

Afterward, the elders wash and wrap the wound with special herbs. The children shower with water and powerful herbs for purification and protection. Any opening of the body exposes a person to many threats. The children are vulnerable at this time to harmful spirits, illness, and infections.

Healing and Power

The circumcised skin is a powerful, highly charged piece full of nyama, which we use for magical purposes. We dip the skins into water which the initiates drink when they have stomachaches; we dip the dried skin in water three times for boys, and four times for girls. A young woman may use her skin for special powers. Her family will prepare her skin with special herbs to protect her from any man who attempts to be intimate with her before she is ready. In some villages, we bury the circumcised skin near a house or in the field. This effort serves as a symbol of the unity between the initiate and the earth.

Village Excursions

While in the bush, the male initiates make visits to the village on Fridays and ask for food. When the young men enter the village periodically, they play their special instruments. Sometimes, during their visit, they leave money on the street and hide. If an elder picks up the trap, he is caught and has to return it with more money. If the elder chooses to run with it, the initiates chase him, singing and dancing. Before returning to the bush, the boys take a chicken, lamb, or goat from someone's farm for dinner. When an animal is missing after a visit from the initiates, we know we are making an offering for their rite of passage.

The young men do not offer their hands to shake until they finish their initiation; they offer their instruments to shake instead. On the day an initiate returns home, he may break his special instrument at the crossroads. In many villages, the initiate will save his ornament like a souvenir, or give it to future initiates for their rites of passage.

Homecoming

At the end of the initiation, the villagers place new clothes in a wagon and send them out to the initiates. The young adults wear these special clothes for a short period upon their return to the village. Our young men wear all white, and our young women wear all black. White symbolizes purity and cleanliness. Black, the color of rich, dark soil and rain clouds, symbolizes fertility and beauty.

When our initiates return from their rite of passage, they may perform the fire dance. The day of their return, friends and family gather along the sidelines and wave little twigs as the initiates run down the path toward a burning fire. The congregation strikes the initiates with their twigs as the initiates make their way toward the fire. The initiates then jump over the fire, repeating this whole procedure three times.

This ceremony symbolizes the initiate's ability to overcome the challenges of the circumcision and his or her entrance into adulthood. The congregation of loved ones symbolically beating the initiates with their sticks reflects the journey that is undertaken alone without the support of friends or family during the initiation. The celebration ends with singing and dancing throughout the night. Our initiates now experience a complete transformation of their roles in the community, and are afforded more respect and more responsibility. The parents sing to their children over and over, "You are brave." Their children, in return, sing a song:

> Thank you to all my mothers,
> Thank you to all my mothers,
> Thank you to all my mothers who are blessed,
> Thank you for all the things you do for us, bring to us and
> give to us,
> Morning and night-time,
> Respect for you.
> There is no crying and no sadness,
> Only all the things you do for us, bring to us and give to us.

13
MARRIAGE

*Your action might have an impact
like that of a baobab seed.*

Marriage is a sacred rite of passage that involves the
entire village. Marriage enables us to perform our
duties and responsibilities to the community. We
marry to have children, who secure the future of
our family's lineage. Our children take care of us
when we are older and they provide us a proper
burial to ensure our transition into the realm of the
ancestors. We choose a mate who best helps us to
fulfill our obligations to our community and to
honor our sacred traditions.

When one is not connected to Spirit, one often
looks to other people and other things to fill that loss
and disconnection. We believe this is a highly dangerous and destructive way to view marriage. We
love our spouses, but they do not replace Spirit for
us. They do not determine our ultimate happiness

or satisfaction. To place that burden of responsibility on another individual will likely cause a cessation of that relationship.

Divorce is rare in our communities, and we believe it is because we are very clear about the meaning and role of marriage. Divorce between two people disrupts the entire community as two or more families have come together to share their lives. When severe challenges arise in a marriage, separation is a common practice, allowing the couple time and space to heal and consult with community members about repairing the marriage.

Marriage serves to bond us together, produce children, and provide care for our elders. Marriage is a community endeavor and a spiritual practice. We come together as a community to worship, pass along our traditions, and honor our ancestors. Usually, for our marriage to be complete, we must raise children together. Our children carry our knowledge about how to live harmoniously with nature and one another. Most importantly, our children receive communication from us when we pass on from the realm of Spirit about how to relate with the spirits effectively and live in our communities peacefully.

Signs of a Spouse

How people talk, walk, and stand tells us many things about who they are and if they will make suitable partners to marry. Traditionally, one would send a friend or family member to observe the actions of a potential spouse. The first observance of a partner is crucial. If a man sends someone to visit a possible mate and he first witnesses her brushing and making up her hair, this is an unfavorable sign. If the woman is sleeping, cooking, or cleaning, these are favorable signs, as they reveal that this is a wife who will be able to relax as well as make her contributions to a functional household. Similarly, if a woman sends a friend or family member to check up on a potential spouse, and he is not home three times in a row, this is not a man who is husband material.

Those who often clasp their hands between their legs will not make tasty food. Those among us who kick up dirt or sand when they walk may be reckless with finances. Those who sway their hands and arms when walking will bring money to the home. We watch our potential spouses carefully to observe signs that will tell us about their characters.

Announcement

The groom first announces his intentions to marry to his father, uncle, or grandfather. If his elder approves of the arrangement, they meet with the father of the potential bride. Afterward, a gathering of the elders will determine if the arrangement is favorable.

Offerings

The man's family offers kola nuts to their friends and extended family at the time of the announcement. They may then make a second offering of kola nuts to solidify the agreement. A third offering of kola nuts can occur the day of the marriage or the day of the announcement for the exact date of the marriage. The groom may also give chewing tobacco, palm wine, or some other kind of liquor to the community. These are gifts we accept, even if we do not use or consume them.

Preparation

Weddings take place any season of the year, though we usually prefer the dry season. A bounty of fish is available during this time, and the weather is better for outdoor festivities. One month before the marriage the engaged couple will have an all-night party, which may last every night for an entire month before the ceremony. Each night, the drummers play different rhythms and the dancers enjoy many dances at the parties. The celebration may include the music of the balafon and the kora.

Before the marriage, the groom's family must save a lot of money, as he will pay for the marriage. The bride's family may contribute, also, though it is not expected. Usually the bride's family and friends will give her presents to start her on her new life, such as a new calabash, a soap dish, clothes, and jewelry. The man will sacrifice at least two animals, such as two cows, or one cow and a lamb, or a cow and a goat. He pays for the animals and his family performs the sacrifice on the morning of the marriage.

A woman will shower with herbs for blessings and protection on the day of her ceremony. Clothed in only a *lapa*, she sits on a mortar as the women sing and the men play the drums at a distance. The women mix the water with the herbs in a new calabash and bathe the bride together. They wash her with a combination of medicinal plants such as kunjé, jala, and kolobé. Kunjé is to protect the bride from harmful spirits, jala is to protect her from illness and misfortune, and kolobé is to protect her from harmful mystical practices others may devise against her. As the women bathe the new bride, they sing and clap:

Wash her,
Wash her clean,
Wash the first lady,
Wash her clean.

In this popular premarital song, the women sing of a ritual cleansing, telling the bride-to-be that they are washing her clean of her childhood. The bride-to-be is no longer a single woman, but receives a new status as a married woman.

Ceremony

The day of the marriage, all of the family and friends arrive. The village leader is ready to perform the sacred union. As the music plays, the bride arrives first with her family. She sits on the floor in front of the village elder, and her husband joins them thereafter. The village elder begins the ceremony by telling the couple how they must live together, how they must respect, help, and love one another in their marriage. To solidify the commitment, the village elder may break kola nuts, pray, and then offer the nuts to the couple to eat. If the couple practices a particular religious faith, they will place their hands on a sacred text and exchange their vows.

Wedding Celebration

Immediately after the exchange of vows, the drums sound and the bard begins to sing. There may be up to five bards at the ceremony, representing each family, and singing the praises of the couple's ancestors. Every day, for up to a month, the couple and their community will continue to drum, dance, and make sacrifices.

Traditionally, it may take up to three months after the wedding before a woman will move into her husband's home. For the next three months the wife will not do any hard work. Afterward, she will begin tending to the household, making a garden, and starting a family. The couple will also visit with the wife's family regularly.

Multiple Marriages

The practice of multiple marriages is a traditional practice that continues to this day. We observe two types of multiple marriages in our communities.[1] The first arrangement is where women share a husband and there is agreement and cooperation among all members about the union. Some women agree to an arrangement of sharing a man who can support a large family. These women enjoy living among other women with whom they raise their children and share in household responsibilities, especially when the husband works in the city and is often away from the home. Sometimes, the husband may take one wife with him when he is away for his work. Infidelity is a serious offense in our communities, as the pregnancy from such a union creates a grave disruption in the harmony and bond already existing between the two families. Many among us believe that multiple marriages help to prevent this kind of disruption.

When a woman is not able to conceive, she often appreciates the opportunity to raise children with cowives, as she will consider these children as her own. As marriage and parenthood are important experiences for the individual to fulfill his or her communal and spiritual roles in Mande life, multiple marriages serve to keep these traditions intact. In the past, during times of war, multiple marriages were especially helpful when the population of men was much lower than the population of women.

The second kind of arrangement is where a man marries more than one wife without the full agreement of all members of the union, which creates disruption in the household. Many women make arrangements with their husbands, before they marry, that they will not take any more wives. Sometimes it is most difficult for the first wife if her husband marries another woman without her consent. Tensions can arise in a household where one or all of the wives are not content with the arrangement. The children of these marriages may suffer from the different treatment they receive from their parents.

We describe two qualities that arise in our children born of these two types of marriages; they are *badenya* and *fadenya*. Badenya means "mother childness," and refers to the affection and loyalty that exists between siblings of the same mother and same father. Fadenya refers to the competitiveness and rivalry that often exists between siblings of the same father but different mothers. The children, who share the same father but different mothers, may develop aggressive dispositions to compete for the resources of their father. Badenya children often have more gentle and docile temperaments. We value and encourage all of these qualities in our communities, and most of us possess a little of each within our personalities.

Many of the powerful shamans in our communities, including the artisans, sometimes manifest more of a fadenya personality, and command fear among members of the community. Excessive aggressiveness is dangerous, though, and we caution our children against developing this trait to an extreme.

We tell the story of Sanjé, to show the challenges that can come with multiple marriages and the unequal treatment of children that may arise. These arrangements can produce an excessive amount of fadenya, resulting in conflicts within the household.

The Story of Sanjé: Without Mother

One time long ago, in a village, there lived a man and his two wives, Soumalé and Kunjé. Both Soumalé and Kunjé each had a daughter, eight-year-old Sanjé and seven-and-a-half-year-old Dibijé. Three days after Sanjé's ninth birthday, her mother passed on. Soumalé was unhappy with Kunjé's special treatment as a wife, and died of a broken heart. Kunjé did not treat Soumalé's daughter like her own, as Soumalé had with Kunjé's daughter.

One year after Soumalé's death, Kunjé begins to treat Sanjé even more unfairly, controlling everything she does and making her work very hard. When Sanjé tells her father of this, Kunjé denies it and immediately punishes Sanjé. Kunjé decides to make life more difficult for Sanjé, and plays a game with her when it is time to eat. She tells the two daughters that whoever cleans and dries her hands first may eat. She offers one bowl of oil to Sanjé to wash her hands in, and a bowl of water to Dibijé. Both girls clean their hands; Sanjé with oil and Dibijé with water. Kunjé tells the children that they must wait for their hands to dry before they come to eat the food. Of course, Sanjé's hands never dry.

Three days in a row, Kunjé makes Sanjé wash her hands with oil, and for three days, Sanjé does not eat. Sanjé is scared to tell her father, for fear that she will again be punished. On the fourth day, after Sanjé finishes her chores, she decides to go to her mother's grave to pray. When she arrives, to her surprise, she finds a gigantic ntoro tree growing right in front of her mother's grave. The tree is full of ripe, juicy fruit, but the tree is so big, and the fruit is so high up that Sanjé cannot reach the branches. Feeling so weak from hunger, Sanjé begins to cry and sing:

> *Come down, come down, ntoro tree,*
> *Come down for the one who doesn't have a mother, ntoro,*
> *Come down for the one who doesn't have a father, ntoro,*
> *They clean one hand with oil and the other hand with water,*
>   *and say the one who will be dry first will eat,*
> *Come down, come down, ntoro,*
> *Come down for the one who doesn't have a mother, ntoro,*
> *Come down for the one who doesn't have a father, ntoro.*

Before Sanjé finishes her song, the gigantic ntoro tree spreads its branches all the way down to the ground around her, as if it is giving Sanjé a big hug. Surrounded by branches full of ripe fruit all around her, Sanjé begins to pick the fruit and eat until she is full. After she finishes, Sanjé prays and returns home.

When Kunjé asks Sanjé where she has been, she tells her she went to her mother's grave to pray. "I am going to my mother's grave every day after I finish my work," she tells Kunjé. Kunjé does not like this, but she cannot prevent her from going if she finishes all of her work.

Every day, Sanjé visits her mother's grave and eats from the ntoro tree and prays, and every day, Sanjé gets stronger, healthier, and more beautiful. In fact, Sanjé begins to see things other people do not see and understand things people around her cannot understand. She becomes so powerful that she is able to see any harmful thing that is going to happen in the house; she is the one who protects her family. Eventually, Sanjé is old enough to leave her home and start her own family. Sanjé lives a blessed life until a ripe old age.

Lessons from the Story of Sanjé

Sanjé's story teaches us that multiple marriages come with many challenges, and if any of the wives are not satisfied and comfortable in the arrangement, disharmony and conflict will arise in the household. In West Africa, it is customary for us to care for the children who do not have a mother or father better than we care for our own children. Sanjé did not receive the love and support from her family that she needed, but she prevails, for it is her ancestors and the spirits who ultimately care for her. Sanjé does not exhibit aggressive behavior toward her family members, though she does pursue her own path. She follows her traditions and receives blessings for her perseverance, stamina, and strength. Sanjé combines fadenya and badenya gracefully.

When Sanjé asks for the ntoro tree to bend down for her, she is following our tradition of respectfully asking the tree for its fruit before taking from it. Sanjé upholds the teachings of her elders by honoring her ancestors, and for this she receives great mystical knowledge and unique abilities. Sanjé continues to respect her family, her ancestors, and the spirits, and in the face of her challenges, she receives what she needs.

14
DEATH &
FUNERALS

The world is full of mysteries.
Not everything can be seen,
but everything exists.

Meaning

Death is not the end of life, but a transformation of it. It is a profound crossing over of the soul from this world into the next. When we pass on, we become ancestors, residing close to Spirit. Crossing over is the final and grandest initiation we make on our life journeys. All of our initiations, teachings, and lessons are preparation for this final moment where we experience our most significant rite of passage. We now have more influence, more power, and more insight to guide and instruct those who remain embodied. When we cross over, we are able to promote the well-being, the unity, and the peace of the community. Many of us believe in a reincarnation of the spirit. Each time we cross over, Spirit keeps a piece of our soul until we are eventually fully united with Spirit.

Pronouncement

Some of us give the dying a glass of water with a prayer before they cross over. We often communicate during this time through drum, dance, song, and conversation with the spirit itself. The community may learn of a death through the drum. The moment there is a declaration of death, we observe silence in the presence of the deceased until after we clean the body. Afterward, we express our range of emotions wholeheartedly. Our outward expressions of mourning can last for months.

Preparation

We take great care in cleaning and preparing the body, bathing it with special herbs. The cleansing can last up to three days. We dress the body in fine clothing and shoes, maybe even a hat and sunglasses. We may place the body in a chair or at the bedside for everyone in the community to come and visit. We construct and prepare the coffin. We prepare the grave and may leave a stick of wood in the grave as a notice to any other wandering spirit not to occupy the site.

Burial

It is important that when one crosses over, it occurs in one's own country or town. We often attempt to bury the body where the person was born. If a loved one passes on outside of the village, we will provide the corpse with a magical object to carry, to help him or her walk home. Many among us bury our loved ones the first, third, seventh, or fortieth day after their transition. We give much thought to our burial places, and we never cremate the bodies. Traditionally, we wrapped the body in white cloth, or in mud cloth, and placed it in the ground without a coffin. Some of us bury our loved ones behind our compound or house. Others of us bury our departed in the sacred baobab tree. Most of us move the body to a burial place some distance away. The coffin is taken to the grave, sometimes in the nearby forest.

We place importance on what our loved ones must wear. We think about the food or supplies they need to take with them. We add money, food, and drink inside the coffin. Sometimes we lay gifts inside the burial case for our ancestors. Many of us place the branch of the ntoro tree, the tree of abundance and rebirth, inside the coffins of our loved ones. We see death as a voyage, and we must properly prepare our loved ones for their travels to the sacred realm. Death is a journey that we are mindful to prepare for throughout our lives, through our actions and behavior.

In carrying the coffin to the grave, we do not carry it through the village street but by the rear of the houses. Carrying the body through the village can create all kinds of difficulties, such as crop failure and supply shortages. During the carrying of the body, people in the community must not move about from place to place, but must remain at the spot where they were when the coffin passed, until the burial is complete. Women with small children must not travel along the same route where we carry the coffin so they will not become ill.

We face the head of the body toward the east when we lay it in the ground. We observe silence as we rest the body into the earth. We may pour libation on the coffin before we cover it with soil. We pour libation onto the ground. After the work of the burial, the men may bathe in a body of water, such as a lake or river, to clean themselves with water for purification after digging the grave. Anything that we use for the burial, such as the wood on which the body was carried, we leave near the grave. These objects contain potent levels of nyama and are dangerous for the living.

Ceremony

We sing, we dance, we cry, and we celebrate. We cry for the loss of the physical presence of our loved ones; we celebrate their new exalted status in the sacred realm of the ancestors.

Some of us may shave our heads and leave our hair at the door of the deceased. Those of us mourning wear black, or in some communities we wear red. Some of us mark our faces with ashes or chalk, and others of us write with chalk on the walls of our homes. Pregnant women and mothers with young children are vulnerable to the high levels of nyama during this time and keep a distance from the center of the mourning and ceremonies. In our songs and prayers we recount the greatness of our ancestor. We may bring gifts to the family to show our love and support.

Every year or few years, we hold a ceremony to honor those who have crossed over. We may clean the cemetery. Sometimes we sacrifice a chicken at the crossroads upon the passing of our loved ones, signaling the changes we are experiencing.

15
WEST AFRICAN
SPIRITUALITY

One never finishes knowing Self.

Through our every thought, deed, and action we aim to serve Spirit. We do not set aside only one day, but make every day a day for worship. Spirit keeps us mindful by communicating to us through the symbols of creation. We take responsibility for our actions and learn from their consequences, which revisit us through the many signs of nature and our environment. Living with a spiritual sensitivity enables us to maintain a positive outlook where we view challenges as opportunities to better understand how to maintain harmony within the universe.

As Spirit reveals itself all around us, we are conscious of the work we engage in, the relationships we maintain, and the rituals we create. We are mindful to optimize peaceful and harmonious energy around us. As we believe that everything is connected, we desire to act wisely and compassionately. To do otherwise is to create a disruption in the balance of the cosmos, which affects all of us. Everything has nyamic repercussions.

As we monitor every symbol and every dream, we realize there is much more to life than appears. We stay present in the little things as much as possible, recognizing that all interactions are meaningful. Opening ourselves to the signs opens up our dialogue with the spirits. We aim to cultivate a spiritual ingenuity recognizing synchronicity, coincidence, and the messages all around us. We strive to know ourselves and our special roles in the universe.

Ultimately, our goal is self-mastery. Those who possess self-mastery are those who experience internal peace and balance; they are the ones who are not attached to things in this life. Detachment from possessions brings us closer to Spirit. Those among us who are not talkative but contemplative, those who are not impulsive but reserved, are those who become the masters of Self.

At the same time we value the ability to surrender. We surrender to the ebb and flow of life, and cultivate an ability to both yield to and direct the life force. We strive to maintain harmony with the rhythms of the universe. This comes through a recognition that the physical is not separate from Spirit. We have the sense of belonging to a whole with which we are all connected. We recognize the immanent presence of Spirit in all things and in all places.

As we are all connected, it is essential to realize that our spiritual progression is both an individual and a communal effort. We share in the celebrations of one another's passages of life.

We mark each phase, each important transition of life with our naming ceremonies, childhood initiations, marriages, and our final journey back to the realm of Spirit. Worshipping together strengthens our ties to the spirit world and to one another.

When we encounter challenges in our lives, we look within the family. If one does not have peace within one's family, one will not have peace in one's life. If we do not show proper respect and appreciation for those who brought us into this world, for those who cared for us, we will not find true contentment. From the family, we explore our role in the community. We look at the contributions we are making and our relationship with those outside of our families. We examine our relationships with our ancestors and the spirits. We ensure that we are showing proper reverence to life, earth, and all of her creatures through regular prayer, sacrifice, and ritual. We consider if we are bringing harm to our environment through careless life choices that invite disruptive nyama into our path. We work to create healing and regenerative energy. We look within, and we also, importantly, look outside of ourselves, taking responsibility for the effects of our actions on everything around us. We explore our relations with family, friends, community, earth, and spirits.

Suffering among any of us is one of the most powerful signs from the spirit world that we heed seriously. Suffering teaches us patience and motivates us to look at our actions carefully. Experiencing pain helps us to understand how our behaviors influence our quality of life and our interactions with one another. We realize that the balance of the forces of nature depends upon our conduct. Suffering teaches us humility, how to share, and how to feel one another. It reminds us to be grateful for the many blessings that surround us.

We understand that to be rich in spirit is the true measure of a person's wealth. We do not desire material possessions that come at the expense of others or are harmful to our environments. One pays greatly for such possessions that serve to set up barriers to Spirit. Paved roads keep our feet from connecting to earth, artificial lights and tall buildings obstruct the spray of sun rays and moonlight that illuminate the beauty that surrounds us. Noisy machines drown out the voices of nature, our communication with the spirits.

We use the many resources available to us through our plants, animals, bush, and waters to live unobtrusively and wholesomely off the land. We aim to take only what we need, and not more. All of our traditional occupations possess a sacred aspect. Our work is a sacred endeavor aimed to please Spirit. Through prayer, libation, offerings, sacrifice, conscious choices, perceptions of symbol, and divination we retain a healthy relationship with Spirit and a balance within the cosmos.

Beliefs of many faiths have swept through our land. The African spiritual approach allows for the integration of different religious practices with its own. Many among us maintain our traditional beliefs and feel comfortable accommodating ideas from other faiths. Any tradition where Spirit is at the heart of its practice finds its home in Africa.

GLOSSARY OF TERMS

Amulets: the most popular type of African charms made and worn to ward off illness, trouble, and disruptive spirits.

Ancestors: spirits of family members who have crossed over; they are guardian spirits. Ultimately, everyone shares the same ancestors from the beginnings of time.

Animal spirit: protective spirit that comes in the form of any animal, such as a goat, snake or horse, and preserves the village from poverty, hunger, and illness.

Badenya: Bamana term meaning "mother-child-ness." It describes the gentleness and kindness that results between children who share the same mother.

Bafoko: instrument made of a large calabash, loosely covered by a goatskin, formerly played when the soldiers went into battle.

Balafon: wooden xylophone, primarily played by Mande bards. In the story of Sunjata, it is Sumanguru Kante who obtained this instrument from the bush spirits.

Bamana: Mande people and language of the middle Niger valley in West Africa.

Bana (*Ceiba pentandra*): strong, powerful trees with many purposes in the village. They are symbols of the legendary Modi Bouramani.

Baobab (*Adansonia digitata*): the most sacred tree of Africa, supplying a host of products including food, water, shelter, clothing, medicine, tools, cosmetics, paper, and charm ingredients.

Balanza (*Acacia albida*): symbol of the male component of creation that connects the heavens and the earth. Women make offerings of shea butter at this tree, which eases their birthing labor.

Bara: see *jansa*.

Bards: preservers of social customs, values and traditions. They are professional historians, storytellers, poets, musicians, and mediators. Masters of verbal, musical, and memory skills, they recite long stories, epics, and praise poems celebrating the African legacy.

Blacksmiths: artisans who produce many of the tools and objects for work, play, defense, ceremony and ritual. They maintain deep relationships with the spirits, and possess great nyamic power.

Bolon: instrument with three strings and a gourd resonator, played as both a harp and a drum. Formerly a war instrument that led soldiers into battle, this instrument is often played at naming ceremonies.

Bush spirits: whimsical spirits of the wilderness, who can transform themselves into anything to serve their purposes.

Calabash: the shell of an inedible fruit used as a container for food and libations, or as a gourd for musical instruments.

Charms: objects or devices that, when consecrated, can bring about the results of specified intentions. See *amulets* and *talismans*.

Circumcision: a rite performed on children as a part of their initiation into adulthood.

Crossroads' spirit: spirit of change, transformation, and protection, found at any crossroads where one may pay homage or leave behind an offering.

Dala: Guinean rhythm that honors fisherwomen.

Denbadon: rhythm that brings together several rhythms and dances to honor mothers.

Diviner: one who sees into the realm of Spirit; diviners may use many objects in nature to aid them in their visions.

Divination: the practice of seeing into the past, present, or future and discovering any mystical or hidden knowledge.

Dogon: people closely related to the Bamana, inhabiting the central regions of Mali.

Dundunba: rhythm from Guinea that honors the strong and the brave. There are more than fifty dundunba rhythms.

Dwarf spirits: wise, mischievous spirits of the bush who sometimes like to surprise and trick people. They are generally harmless spirits who have much to teach.

Fadenya: Bamana term for "father-childness," that refers to the competition and rivalry that exists between siblings who share the same father but different mothers.

Faro: Bamana spirit of the waters and specifically of the Niger River. Faro is represented as a feminine or androgynous divinity, depending on the context.

Frankincense: fragrant gum resin burnt in West Africa, primarily for protection and to ward away disruptive or harmful spirits.

Gambia: modern state in West Africa, inhabited largely by the Mandinka, a Mande people.

Gourds: shells of inedible fruits used as instrument pieces, and vessels or containers for food or herbs.

Guinea: a modern republic of West Africa with a large population of Mande speakers.

Healer see *shaman.*

Hunters: powerful healers and members of the community, who work in the realm of wilderness animals and spirits. Hunters learn about the different plants and animals of the forest, and how to use this knowledge to be powerful healers as well.

Incantation: a formula of sacred words chanted or recited over an object, person, or situation to consecrate it.

Initiations: rites and ceremonies that confer a special status upon the initiate in the community. Initiations are integral to the growth and development of individuals within a society.

Initiation societies: also known as secret societies, are groups that members of the community belong to where they receive some of the highest forms of knowledge, learn to master forces of the visible and invisible world, and often submit to tests of endurance, courage, and intelligence.

Invocation: the petitioning of a spirit or spirits for help or support.

Jala (*Khaya senegalensis*): popular herb used as an internal cleanser or energy booster. It is also a protective herb that children both wear and consume when they are ill. Adults bathe with this herb to ward off illness and misfortune.

Jansa: also known as **bara**, is a Malian rhythm for many celebrations, especially for the full moon, spring equinox, summer and winter solstices, weddings, and harvest celebrations.

Jembé: one of the most common drums found throughout West Africa, originating from the Mali and Guinea regions. Jembé means to come together and share the music in the Bamana language.

Jembéfola: a master jembé player.

Jun-juns (also known as **dun-duns**): large two-headed drums made of wood and cow-skin that often accompany jembé playing, providing the bass of the music. The kinkini is the smallest of the three jun-juns, the sangwa is the medium-sized drum, and the jun-jun is the largest of them all.

Kakilambé: Baga Guinean rhythm that honors the spirit Kakilambé, housed in a sacred mask of the Baga people, and protector against disruptive spirits. This rhythm is also a welcoming song and dance.

Kalakari (*Heeria insignis*): tree of luck, known to respond to one's petitions.

Kassa: also known as **susu,** is a traditional harvest dance and rhythm of the Malinké people.

Kinkini: the smallest of the three jun-jun drums.

Kola nuts: edible nuts that serve as medicine, offerings, gifts, and divination aids. Kola, which contains high levels of caffeine, is a stimulant.

Kolobé or **kinkéliba** (*Combretum micranthum*): popular West African tea consumed daily for general well-being. It is a diuretic and helps to speed up the healing process when one is ill.

Komo: a drum rhythm and a sacred mask dance of the blacksmiths. Komadon is the dance of the powerful secret society komo. This rhythm helps to heal those who experience spirit possessions or mental challenges.

Kontron: the Bamana hunters' masculine divinity, often paired with Sanènè.

Kora: a harp-like instrument made of a calabash gourd cut in half and partially covered with cow skin. It usually has twenty-one playing strings.

Koreduga: Malian rhythm played for the koreduga, a Bamana caste whose role it is to make the crowd laugh by using mimicry and acrobatics during festivities and celebrations.

Kunjé (*Guiera senegalensis*): popular protective herb utilized to keep away disruptive spirits. This herb is also an effective remedy for coughs and toothaches.

Kuku: Guinean rhythm traditionally performed for boy initiates who returned from their circumcision ritual. It is now played for all types of celebrations.

Laka: or porridge, is a popular offering that consists of a cooked grain, such as millet, and the sauce, which can be made as a separate offering. The sauce consists of yogurt, milk, and sugar.

Lamba: dance and drum rhythm played at major rites of passage ceremonies.

Libation: liquid offering we make to the realm of Spirit, most often including palm wine, millet beer, and water.

Liberté: also known as **ligueba**, is a Guinea rhythm celebrating Guinea's independence from French rule. Liberté is popular at festivals and is a competition rhythm for ballet schools.

Mali: modern republic of West Africa and homeland of the Mande founded by Sunjata Keita in the thirteenth century.

Malinké: people of the Mande, populated in the regions of Mali and Guinea.

Mande: large West African language family and homeland, covering the regions of Mali, Gambia, Guinea, Guinea Bissau, Burkina Faso, Ivory Coast, Senegal and parts of Liberia, Mauritania, and Sierra Leone.

Mandesunsun (*Annona senegalensis*): herbal remedy for arthritis, mental illnesses, pregnancy complications, and impotence.

Mandinka: people of the Mande, populated mostly in the regions of Gambia.

Manjani: Mande rhythm from the border of Mali and Guinea, played at festive occasions. Manjani is also an initiation and celebration dance.

Maraka: marriage and baptism rhythm originating in Mali.

Modi Bouramani: an historical figure who protects initiates undergoing circumcision by keeping away harmful spirits. The seben and bana trees are symbols of Modi Bouramani.

Moribiassa: rhythm played for very specific occasions, such as the return of a special person not seen in many years, whether they are a living individual or an ancestor. This rhythm is also danced by women at the crossroads to pray for those who are ill.

Mortar: sacred vessel where herbs, charm ingredients, or food are ground and pounded with a pestle.

Mud cloth: sacred, protective garment made by women for the hunters. Women also wear mud cloth during prominent times in their lives, including after the birth of their first child, after menopause, and at their burial.

Muso Koroni: Bamana mother of creation, chaos, and mystical practices. Muso Koroni translates to "old woman spirit." This dominant spirit is all the more powerful because of her crone status. In her personification of air and fire, she is known as Nyalé.

Naming ceremony: ceremony performed one week after the birth of a child, where the name of the newborn is announced to the community.

Neem (*Azadirachta indica*): plant used worldwide for numerous healing purposes; neem is an antibacterial, antiviral, antiseptic herb that strengthens the immune system.

Ndomayiri: divine ancestor of all blacksmiths and extraordinary shaman who represents the element of earth.

Ngoni: ancient traditional lute found throughout West Africa that usually has either four or seven strings.

Ngrin: mother of all the rhythms originating from Mali, played for festive occasions such as marriage and naming ceremonies, and for healers and diviners.

Nponponpogolon (*Calotropis procera*): tree whose inedible fruit is a helpful protective charm and brings prosperity and abundance.

Ntomi (*Tamarindus indica*): also known as tamarind juice, is a popular drink with medicinal uses for numerous ailments, including constipation, ulcers, impotence, fever, and asthma.

Ntoro (*Ficus capensis*): remedy for many ailments, especially arthritis, infertility, and illnesses during pregnancy. This tree symbolizes abundance and rebirth.

Nyama: the energy of Spirit that flows throughout the universe. It is the life force that links everything together.

Nya gwan: an extraordinary being, the superhealer, who comes into the world complete with powerful potential. Nya gwan is also a powerful secret society for women.

Nyalé: Bamana divinity, also known as Muso Koroni, that represents the spirit of air and fire in Bamana cosmology.

Occult: the secretive, hidden, or mysterious. It refers to practices that engage the supernatural realm.

Offering: that which is given as a prayer, amend, or gift to the spirits.

Palm wine: a milky, alcoholic beverage collected by tapping palm trees. It is often poured for libations and served on festive occasions.

Pendelou: the underskirts worn only by married women.

Pestle: club-shaped sacred tool used to pound and grind charm ingredients, herbs, and food in a mortar.

Rituals: ceremonial acts performed to honor or communicate with the realm of Spirit.

Roselle (*Hibiscus sabdariffa*): popular food beverage and medicine with many internal and external applications. This herb remedies colds, constipation, urinary infections, circulation disorders, sores, and wounds.

Sabar: set of drums, rhythms, and dances of the Wolof people of Senegal. Sabar rhythms speak the languages of the Wolof and Serer peoples.

Sacrifice: that which one makes as a prayer, amend, or gift to the spirits.

Sangwa (also pronounced "sangba"): the medium-sized drum of the set of three jun-juns.

Sanènè: the Bamana hunters' feminine divinity often paired with Kontron.

Seben (*Borassus aethiopum*): strong, powerful tree with many purposes in the community. It is a symbol of Modi Bouramani, the protector of circumcised initiates.

Senegal: modern republic of West Africa, populated largely by the Wolof people.

Shamans: divinely inspired people with high concentrations of nyama. They possess the ability to direct this energy for a multitude of purposes, including healing, charm making, and divination. They also often have abilities to convene with various spirits and divine their intentions.

Shea butter: oil from the nut of a sweet, edible fruit that is both consumed and used as a healing product. It also has uses for instruments, spiritual cleanses, and ritual purposes.

Soko: Guinean rhythm for uninitiated children during the months preceding the male rite of circumcision.

Soli: Guinean rhythm, performed mostly for the circumcisions of boys and girls.

Soliwulén: red panther that is in charge of protecting young boys and girls in the days before their adulthood initiation.

Sorsoner: rhythm that comes from the Baga people of Guinea. Young girls dance this rhythm in the full moonlight to show respect for their mothers.

Soso: region and people of Guinea once ruled by Sumanguru Kante.

Spirit: the One, ultimate unifying principal and Creator of the universe.

Spirits: intermediaries for Spirit.

Spirit abode: dwelling place for a spirit. It is usually an object sacrificed to regularly that takes the form of a sculpture or a mask. This is not an object for worship, but instead is home to a spirit that one communicates with regularly.

Spirit possession: experience of a spirit *invading* a person's body uninvited. It often requires the intervention of spirit mediums to release the possessing force and divine the reason for the possession.

Spirit visitation: inhabitation of an individual by an invited spirit. The spirit often provides healing and imparts knowledge for those present.

Sumanguru Kante: thirteenth-century Soso leader who lost the Mande kingdom to Sunjata Keita.

Sunjata Keita: thirteenth-century king who united the Mande kingdom.

Sunu: Malian rhythm that honors Sunu Mamady, a skilled dancer. Sunu is also a rhythm for traditional feast days, marriages, and other festivals.

Talismans: charms that bring things to the owner, such as success and prosperity.

Teliko: masculine divinity of air, or most specifically, of whirlwinds, in Bamana.

Tokho: word that does not have any specific meaning, but is uttered all over West Africa when a baby coughs, to help make the baby strong.

Wassa: divination term used to denote health, longevity, and prosperity. When a diviner performs a reading, such as cowrie shell divination, a favorable configuration is called wassa.

Wolof: language and people of Senegal.

Yankadi: dance and courting rhythm of the Guinean people.

Yo: beginning sound of the universe in Bamana cosmology.

NOTES

Introduction

1. The Mande people, also called Mandinga by many African scholars, include, but are not limited to the Bama-na, Mandinka, Maninka, Mandingo, Malinké, Manya, Jula, Kuranko, Soninke, and Wangara.

Chapter 1

1. Spirits are equivalent to what are perceived as angels and devils in many of the world religions.

2. The belief in a life-force energy that permeates the universe is a concept found in many traditions all over the world. Nyama is a highly developed version of the vital force that incorporates a moral component. Comparable to notions found in Eastern traditions, nyama is a life-force energy that flows throughout the universe like chi, while espousing moral repercussions like karma. Nyama is similar to other concepts in West African traditions, such as ashé among the Yoruba.

3. "Shaman" is a word we propose to replace terms such as "sorcerer" and "witch doctor," as these titles have been viewed in a derogatory manner. It should be noted that in the Mande vocabulary there are many titles given to those who work in the realm of Spirit, including but not limited to: "wise persons," "masters of secret things," "masters of medicine," and "persons who know." Among these specialists there are often those who belong to more than one category. As they all work with mystical energy and spirits, and often for healing purposes, the term shaman seems the most suitable label.

4. Animal spirit is equivalent to what is known as a totem in indigenous cultures around the world.

5. The only time a community will kill an animal spirit is for a ritual sacrifice, which takes place in some villages every seven years. At this time the animal spirit is sacrificed and a new animal spirit will replace it. Before the animal is sacrificed, the elders will bring together the heads of both animals to transfer the nyama of the old spirit into the new one.

6. This story is only one version of many on the origination of the name Couloubaly.

7. Bush spirits are known as *jinn* in the Islamic traditions.

8. Dwarf spirits are similar to the dwarves, elves, and leprechauns of European traditions, which also share a special connection to nature. Though dwarf spirits tend to look more like the dwarves of the European traditions, they are most like the leprechauns in their abilities and characteristics. Dwarf spirits are also like the bogeys, pixies, and fairies of European traditions that range up to nearly two feet and enjoy playing tricks on people.

9. Existing literature on the topic of these spirits has misclass-ified them as "witches," with the misinformed notion of a witch being an evil, destructive (usually female) individual. These disruptive spirits are most closely aligned with dem-ons and succubi spirits in traditions worldwide.

Chapter 2

1. Animal sacrifice has been an important practice of indige-nous traditions all over the world, since the beginnings of time. Animal sacrifice has also been, historically, an integral component of some of the world religions, such as Judaism, Islam, and Christianity.

2. We call this dish *laka*.

Chapter 3

1. Cowrie shells come from the ocean, and have round backs and flat stomachs, like the shape of a round nut cut in half. On the flat of the surface they have a jagged split or opening down the center. Their resemblance to female genitalia has made them a sacred symbol for fertility rites and other ritual purposes in many indigenous cultures. They also have been used historically as money through-out Africa for centuries, symbolizing wealth and power.

2. The word "bard" itself is not traditionally a complete de-scription of what one refers to as a *griot*, or a *jeli/jali* in Mande cultures. In this work, we are redefining bard, as did the Nigerian government, to include its many roles, such as historian, musician, storyteller, and preserver of customs, values, and traditions.

3. The divine ancestor of all blacksmiths and extraordinary shaman is Ndomayiri, who represents the element of earth.

4. Iron is held to be a sacred substance in many cultures worldwide. Wiccan traditions especially make use of iron ritual objects. Iron runs throughout our blood, the earth, and our solar system. It is a basic substance of nature and an essential ingredient for our cultural tools and objects.

5. Many women also wear mud cloth during prominent times in their lives, including the periods after the birth of a first child, after menopause, and at their burial. Women share the powerful act of shedding blood (or the notable cessation of it) during these times with the hunter who also sheds a great amount of blood during the hunts. The nyama of the cloth and its symbolism serve as protection and empowerment for women and hunters.

Chapter 4

1. This is a primary example of the karmic aspects of nyama.

2. Seven is a magical number, as it combines the cosmic numbers of man (three) and woman (four) in the Bamana creation story.

3. The need for ritual taboos during a woman's menstruation derives from the Mande's recognition that fertility and motherhood are sacred. A common mistake is to interpret the taboos around menstruation as reflecting a belief that menstruation is unclean or impure. The Mande do not use such terms to refer to menstruation. To truly grasp the consecrated nature of menstruation, in the Mande world, is to understand the need for ritual regulation to contain and honor its power.

4. In many indigenous cultures, red clay (rich in iron ore) has come to symbolize the blood of birth and is found all over ancient sacred burial sites and ritual objects. White clay, symbolizing purity and clarity, is a thick, compact substance useful for ceremonial markings and spirit abode constructions in many indigenous cultures.

Chapter 5

1. Neem (*Azadirachta indica*) is a favorite herb worldwide, with particular popularity in Ayurveda medicine where it is employed for many ailments, especially chronic ulcers and scabies.

Chapter 6

1. The feminine divinity Nyalé, also known as Muso Koroni—the mother of creation, chaos, and mystical practices—represents the spirit of air and fire in Bamana cosmology. Teliko is the masculine divinity of air or, most specifically, of whirlwinds, in Bamana cosmology.

2. The spirit of water also represents speech.

3. The Bamana spirit of the water is Faro. Faro is a feminine or androgynous divinity, depending on the context. Faro is often represented as a mermaid, with long hair, breasts, and a fishtail. Faro prefers sacrifices of white objects, copper, and tomatoes (representing blood). There is a close link between blood and water in Mande cosmology, both representing the fluids of life.

4. While the earth is generally referred to as mother, her masculine representative is the shaman and ancestor of the blacksmiths, Ndomyiri (master of the trees).

Chapter 7

1. To explore similar beliefs and understandings in African American perceptions of dreams, read *Dream-Singers: The African American Way with Dreams* by Anthony Shafton (John Wiley & Sons, Publ.).

Chapter 10

1. In the Mande tradition, we trace our names to the key figures in the epic of Sunjata, the thirteenth-century king who united the Mande kingdom.

2. Gender roles, in Mande cultures, are clearly defined, and at the same time not. Women do primarily care for the household and cook and tend to the garden. They also are some of the most powerful diviners, healers, and shamans of the community. The largest misconception is that because there is a clear delineation of gender roles in some African societies, women are viewed as inferior. The delineation of gender roles, more than anything, is based on the sacred functions that both men and women hold in the community and their complementary functions with one another.

Chapter 11

1. Muso Koroni translates to "old woman spirit." This dominant spirit in Bamana cosmology is all the more powerful because of her crone status. Muso Koroni's creation of the world would not be complete without her introducing the element of chaos, thus completing the natural cycle of life and death.

2. We call this extraordinary being, the nya gwan, the super healer or shaman. Nya gwan is also a powerful secret society for women in our communities.

3. Among both traditionalists and Muslims, special names are given to twins.

4. This passage explains that the male elders shared with Sira Jan powerful words to use for her protection.

5. Women showing their pendelou, or underskirts, is a rare occurrence; it is a symbol that the women elders entrusted Sira Jan with their most powerful secrets.

6. The young boys carry slingshots to protect Sira Jan from anyone or thing that tries to harm her.

Chapter 12

1. In Islam, children are circumcised at a young age, which may also contribute to the younger age of circumcision spreading in traditional villages.

2. Some African governments have made female circumcision illegal due to pressures from both local and international communities and organizations.

3. If a young boy is not able to undergo circumcision, due to an irregular skin formation that cannot be excised, the circumcisor may produce a cut on the boy's thigh, which is an acceptable substitute for the act of circumcision.

4. Read Griaule and Dieterlen's *The Pale Fox* (Continuum, 1986) to understand the history and significance of the constellations, especially of Sirius and its invisible star.

Chapter 13

1. Multiple marriages in Mande communities can also include one woman marrying a set of twin brothers.

BIBLIOGRAPHY

Amen, Ra Un Nefer. *Metu Neter: The Great Oracle of Tehuti and the Egyptian System of Spiritual Cultivation.* Bronx, NY: Khamit Corporation, 1990.

Appiah, Kwame and Henry Louis Gates Jr. *Africana: The Encyclopedia of the African and African American Experience.* New York: Basic Civitas Books, 1999.

Bâ, Amadou Hampaté. *Aspects de la civilisation africaine: personne, culture, religion.* Paris: Présence africaine, 1972.

Bailleul, Pere Charles. *Dictionnaire Francais-Bambara.* Bamako, Mali: Editions Donniya, 1998.

Belcher, Stephen. *Epic Traditions of Africa.* Bloomington and Indianapolis: Indiana University Press, 1999.

Birnbaum, Lucia Chiavola. *Dark Mother: African Origins and Godmothers.* San Jose, CA: Authors Choice Press, 2001.

Brett-Smith, Sarah Catherine. *The Making of Mande Sculpture: Creativity and Gender.* Massachusetts: Cambridge University Press, 1998.

Charry, Eric. *Mande Music: Traditional and Modern Music of the Maninka and Mandinka of Western Africa.* Chicago: The University of Chicago Press, 2000.

Cissé, Youssouf Tata. *La confrerie des chasseurs Malinké et Bambara: Mythes, rites et recits initiatiques.* Paris: Nouvelles du Sud, 1964.

Conrad, David C., and Barbara E. Frank. *Status and Identity in West Africa: Nyamakalaw of Mandinga.* Bloomington: Indiana University Press, 1995.

Cunningham, Scott. *The Complete Book of Incense, Oils & Brews.* Saint Paul, MN: Llewellyn Publications, 1998.

Davis, Angela Y. *Global Critical Race Feminism: An International Reader.* New York: New York University Press, 2000.

Diallo, Yaya, and Mitchell Hall. *The Healing Drum: African Wisdom Teachings.* Rochester, VT: Destiny Books, 1989.

Dieterlen, Germaine. *Essai sur la religion Bambara.* Paris: Presses Universitaires de France, 1951.

Diop, Cheikh Anta. *The African Origin of Civilization.* New York: Lawrence Hill Books, 1974.

Fisher, Robert B. *West African Religious Traditions: Focus on the Akan of Ghana.* Maryknoll, New York: Orbis Books, 1998.

Gleason, Judith. *Oya: In Praise of an African Goddess.* New York: HarperCollins, 1992.

Griaule, M., and G. Dieterlen. *The Pale Fox.* Chino Valley, AZ: Continuum Foundation, 1986.

Hale, Thomas A. *Griots and Griottes: Masters of Words and Music.* Bloomington and Indianapolis: Indiana University Press, 1998.

Idowu, Bolaji E. *African Traditional Religion: A Definition.* Maryknoll, NY: Orbis Books, 1973.

Imperato, Pascal James. *African Folk Medicine: Practices and Beliefs of the Bambara and Other Peoples.* Baltimore: York Press, 1977.

——. *Legends, Sorcerers, and Enchanted Lizards: Door Locks of the Bamana of Mali.* New York: Africana Pub., 2001.

Kraig, Donald Michael. *Modern Magick: Eleven Lessons in the High Magickal Arts.* Second edition. St. Paul, MN: Llewellyn Publications, 1988 and 1998.

Magesa, Laurenti. *African Religion: The Moral Traditions of Abundant Life.* Maryknoll, New York: Orbis Books, 1997.

Mbiti, John S. *African Religions and Philosophy.* Portsmouth, NH: Heinemann: A Division of Reed Publishing, 1969.

McNaughton, Patrick R. *The Mande Blacksmiths: Knowledge, Power and Art in West Africa.* Bloomington and Indianapolis: Indiana University Press, 1988.

Nnaemeka, Obioma, editor. *Sisterhood, Feminisms, and Power: from Africa to the Diaspora.* Trenton, NJ: Africa World Press, 1998.

Sargent, Denny. *Global Ritualism: Myth & Magic Around the World.* Saint Paul, MN: Llewellyn Publications, 1994.

Somé, Malidoma Patrice. *The Healing Wisdom of Africa: Finding Life Purpose Through Nature, Ritual, and Community.* New York: Penguin Putnam, Inc. 1998.

Suso, Bamba, and Banna Kanute. *Sunjata: Gambian Versions of the Mande Epic.* New York, NY: Penguin Books, 1974 and 1999.

Tompkins, Peter, and Christopher Bird. *The Secret Life of Plants.* New York: Harper & Row Publishers, 1989.

Wilson, Sule Greg. *The Drummer's Path: Moving the Spirit with Ritual and Traditional Drumming*. Rochester, VT: Destiny Books, 1992.

Zahan, Dominique. *The Bambara*. Leiden: E. J. Brill, 1974.

INDEX

LLEWELLYN ORDERING INFORMATION

Order Online:
Visit our website at www.llewellyn.com, select your books, and order them
on our secure server.

Order by Phone:
- Call toll-free within the U.S. at 1-877-NEW-WRLD
  (1-877-639-9753). Call toll-free within Canada at
  1-866-NEW-WRLD (1-866-639-9753)
- We accept VISA, MasterCard, and American Express

Order by Mail:
Send the full price of your order (MN residents add 7% sales tax) in U.S.
funds, plus postage & handling to:
> **Llewellyn Worldwide**
> **P.O. Box 64383, Dept. 0-7387-0626-4**
> **St. Paul, MN 55164-0383, U.S.A.**

Postage & Handling:
> **Standard** (U.S., Mexico, & Canada). If your order is:
> > Up to $25.00, add $3.50
> > $25.01 - $48.99, add $4.00
> > $49.00 and over, FREE STANDARD SHIPPING
> (Continental U.S. orders ship UPS. AK, HI, PR, & P.O. Boxes ship
> USPS 1st class. Mex. & Can. ship PMB.)

> **International Orders:**
> > **Surface Mail:** For orders of $20.00 or less, add $5 plus $1 per
> > item ordered. For orders of $20.01 and over, add $6 plus $1
> > per item ordered.

> > **Air Mail:**
> > *Books:* Postage & Handling is equal to the total retail price of
> > all books in the order.
> > *Non-book items:* Add $5 for each item.

Orders are processed within 2 business days.
Please allow for normal shipping time. Postage and handling rates subject to change.

Hoodoo Mysteries

Folk Magic, Mysticism & Rituals

Ray Malbrough

An insider reveals the secrets of Hoodoo. Ray Malbrough, author of the best selling *Charms, Spells, and Formulas*, is one of the few hereditary folk magicians raised in Louisiana. In his latest book, he presents a living history of the magico-religious practices of Louisiana Hoodoo, the American cousin of traditional Haitian Voudoo.

Learn how this religious belief survived as it developed within American shores. Explore the different types of divinatory and magical practices still in use today, including spiritual/magical baths, spellwork for individuals and root doctors, the ritual use of the Pot de Tête (Head Pot) and Medium's Necklace, and invocation of the Gédé (spirits of the dead).

0-7387-0350-8, 240 pp., 6 x 9   **$12.95**

Sticks, Stones, Roots & Bones

Hoodoo, Mojo & Conjuring with Herbs

Stephanie Rose Bird

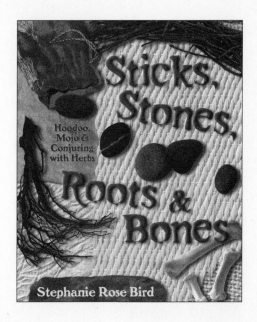

Learn the art of everyday rootwork in the twenty-first century. Hoodoo is an eclectic blend of African traditions, Native American herbalism, Judeo-Christian ritual, and magical healing. Tracing Hoodoo's magical roots back to West Africa, Stephanie Rose Bird provides a fascinating history of this nature-based healing tradition and gives practical advice for applying Hoodoo magic to everyday life. Learn how sticks, stones, roots, and bones—the basic ingredients in a Hoodoo mojo bag—can be used to bless the home, find a mate, invoke wealth, offer protection, and improve your health and happiness.

0-7387-0275-7, 288 pp., 7½ x 9⅛, illus.   **$14.95**

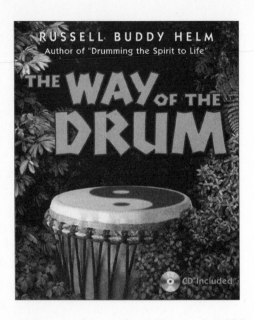

The Way of the Drum

Buddy Helm

"Feeling a groove puts us in a mythic state of passion and personal power. We sense universal mystery and and unnameable magic. It gets our juices flowing and we feel alive … Without our connection to those inspirational animal grooves, our souls turn grey."

These are the words of drummer Buddy Helm, who in fifty short "conversations" shares his discoveries about life through the magical experience of drumming. He integrates insider's stories from the entertainment industry, practical how-tos of drumming technique, tips for improving your own drumming experience, inspiring personal reflections, and unforgettable tales of the healing effects of the drum on people's lives.

Features exercises for trance drumming, tantric sex grooves, and releasing the wounds inflicted from past music teachers The accompanying CD of invocation drumming is a moving example of the points made in the book.

The author is a professional drummer who has played with Frank Zappa, Chuck Berry, Van Morrison, and the Allman Brothers. Included are several stories of celebrities, including how Buddy Helm and Wolfman Jack saved the day at Halloween.

0-7387-0159-9, 360 pp., 7½ x 9⅛, illus., CD included $19.95